Cambridge Elements ≡

Elements in Applied Social Psychology
edited by
Susan Clayton
College of Wooster, Ohio

ENTRAPMENT, ESCAPE, AND ELEVATION FROM RELATIONSHIP VIOLENCE

Wind Goodfriend
*Buena Vista University, Institute for the Prevention
of Relationship Violence*

Pamela Lassiter Simcock
*Harvard University, Institute for the Prevention
of Relationship Violence*

CAMBRIDGE
UNIVERSITY PRESS

University Printing House, Cambridge CB2 8BS, United Kingdom

One Liberty Plaza, 20th Floor, New York, NY 10006, USA

477 Williamstown Road, Port Melbourne, VIC 3207, Australia

314–321, 3rd Floor, Plot 3, Splendor Forum, Jasola District Centre,
New Delhi – 110025, India

103 Penang Road, #05–06/07, Visioncrest Commercial, Singapore 238467

Cambridge University Press is part of the University of Cambridge.

It furthers the University's mission by disseminating knowledge in the pursuit of
education, learning, and research at the highest international levels of excellence.

www.cambridge.org
Information on this title: www.cambridge.org/9781108986809
DOI: 10.1017/9781108981545

© Wind Goodfriend and Pamela Lassiter Simcock 2022

First published 2022

A catalogue record for this publication is available from the British Library.

ISBN 978-1-108-98680-9 Paperback
ISSN 2631-777x (online)
ISSN 2631-7761 (print)

Entrapment, Escape, and Elevation from Relationship Violence

Elements in Applied Social Psychology

DOI: 10.1017/9781108981545
First published online: June 2022

Wind Goodfriend
Buena Vista University, Institute for the Prevention of Relationship Violence

Pamela Lassiter Simcock
Harvard University, Institute for the Prevention of Relationship Violence

Author for correspondence: Wind Goodfriend, goodfriend@bvu.edu

Abstract: How does experiencing intimate partner violence (IPV) affect one's identity in terms of self-concept and self-esteem? This Element proposes a novel framework called the E3 Model in which relevant theory and research studies can be organized into three phases: Entrapment, Escape, and Elevation. Entrapment focuses on how people enter and commit to a relationship that later becomes abusive and how experiencing IPV affects the self. Escape explores how victims become survivors as they slowly build the resources needed to leave safely, including galvanizing self-esteem. Finally, Elevation centers on how survivors psychologically rebuild from their experience and become stronger, happier, more hopeful selves. The Element concludes with a discussion of applications of the E3 Model, such as public and legal policy regarding how to best help and support survivors.

This Element also has a video abstract: www.cambridge.org/AppliedSocialPsychology_Goodfriend_abstract

Keywords: intimate partner violence, relationship abuse, self-concept, self-esteem, identity

ISBNs: 9781108986809 (PB), 9781108981545 (OC)
ISSNs: 2631-777x (online), 2631-7761 (print)

Contents

1 Introduction

Two of the central foci of social psychology are perceptions of the self and of interpersonal relationships. Perhaps there is no greater crucible for one's self-concept and self-esteem than experiencing intimate partner violence (IPV). What happens to the self when the person who is supposed to love and support you the most is the one who harms you?

The World Health Organization defines IPV as "behavior within an intimate relationship that causes physical, sexual, or psychological harm, including acts of physical aggression, sexual coercion, psychological abuse, and controlling behaviors" (2010, p. 11). The frequency of IPV can be surprising and somewhat staggering. Recent statistics estimate that 47 percent of men and women in the United States experience psychological or physical abuse from a partner at least once in their lifetime (National Center for Victims of Crime, 2018). Estimates in other countries vary, but the scope of the issue is difficult to measure due to public stigma aimed toward survivors and, therefore, lack of reporting of IPV to any kind of authority (see Arnocky & Vaillancourt, 2014; Littleton, 2010; Murray et al., 2018). In the worst-case scenario, intimate partners account for about 45 percent of homicides of women in the United States and 5 percent of homicides of men (Cooper & Smith, 2011).

The self-concept is generally defined as the summary of who we are, including our personality, positive and negative traits, experiences, goals, individual and group-based social roles, and more (Bem, 1967; Higgins, 1987; Rivenburgh, 2000; Tajfel, 1981). In contrast, self-esteem is our subjective evaluation of our self-concept; it is our judgment of whether and the degree to which we like who we are (Baumeister et al., 1996; Crocker & Major, 1989; Greenwald et al., 2002). Several scholars in social psychology offer theories regarding how the self-concept and self-esteem are affected by one's intimate relationships. For example, self-expansion theory (Aron & Aron, 1986) notes that people's self-concept often includes their romantic partner, such that our individual talents and experiences can grow when our partner fosters them. Interdependence theory (Kelley & Thibaut, 1978) suggests that decision-making changes once we are in a committed relationship, with selfish motives transforming into a desire to maintain long-term satisfaction for both partners. Cognitive interdependence theory (Agnew et al., 1998) points out that once a solid relationship has formed, individual partners shift from thinking of the self as "me" and "my" to "we" and "our." Work from both behavioral confirmation theory (Darley & Fazio, 1980; Merton, 1948) and the "Michelangelo phenomenon" (Drigotas et al., 1999) note that our partner's expectations of us can slowly affect our self-concept, changing our worldviews and goals for the future.

Given these theoretical foundations, it seems clear that relationship partners have a significant influence on each other's self-concept and self-esteem. Ideally, partners support and encourage each other, leading both to feel the benefits of being together. But the presence of aggression, violence, and psychological, sexual, and/or emotional manipulation in a relationship can change this experience to one of disappointment and degradation. These negative effects may be exacerbated in individuals who also suffer from systemic disadvantages and discrimination because of – for example – status based on their ethnicity (Jaffray, 2021; Rizkalla et al., 2020), being undocumented or a refugee (Njie-Carr et al., 2020), disability (Brownridge et al., 2020; Savage, 2021; Stern et al., 2020), transgender or sexual minority identity (Peitzmeier et al., 2020; Pittman et al., 2020; Scheer et al., 2020), or socioeconomic status (Cunradi et al., 2002; Hammett et al., 2020; Stalans & Ritchie, 2008).

Social psychological theories offer insight into how one's self is transformed through the experience of IPV. Pragmatically, attention to victims and survivors is needed to ameliorate this pervasive societal problem. Academically, more understanding is needed to advance theory and scholarship on the psychological mechanisms involved in IPV relationship dynamics. There is already a well-known model called I^3 (Finkel, 2008, 2014; Finkel & Hall, 2018; Finkel et al., 2012). This model is useful for predicting when interpersonal violence is most likely to occur, including within romantic couples. Instigation (the first "I") refers to immediate aspects of a couple conflict that typically make violence more likely (e.g., jealousy). Impellance is the couple members' personalities that might affect IPV behaviors (e.g., narcissism). Finally, inhibition includes factors that might decrease violence (e.g., self-discipline). While promising in its own right, the I^3 Model does not focus specifically on IPV survivors' psychological experiences and does not offer implications for change in given individuals over time.

We propose the E3 Model to specifically capture the psychological viewpoints and longitudinal experiences of survivors of IPV in terms of their evolving identity, self-concept, and self-esteem. We suggest a novel way to organize relevant research with a three-phase framework: Entrapment, Escape, and Elevation. Each phase highlights how a survivor moves through IPV from start to finish and the possible accompanying changes to one's sense of self. (Note that while Finkel's I^3 Model is typically pronounced "I cubed," we suggest pronouncing our model "E three.")

The E3 Model posits three phases for two reasons. First, it parallels the I^3 model reviewed here. But, much more importantly, many IPV researchers and scholars discuss the experience of survivors in phases but without consistency in formalizing and naming them. One example comes from Rosen (1996; Rosen & Stith, 1997), who interviewed survivors and outlined movement through a seduction period, then "entrapment", then "escape". Heywood et al. (2019) focus on the aftermath of IPV by interviewing women as they shifted from "victim" to "survivor" to "thriver," a model more directly parallel to our own. Others focus exclusively on cross-sectional moments in a relationship (e.g., attraction, escape), many of which are described later, but without emphasis on longitudinal change. We believe the three phases of the E3 Model are intuitive and reflect much of the current work on IPV. In layperson's terms, the phases might be discussed as "getting in, getting out, and healing." That said, we acknowledge that more than three phases might feel right to some survivors, while others might relate to possible subphases and so on. We recognize that each person's experience is individual and valid for them; the E3 Model is intended to suggest what may be common trends for many people – not necessarily all.

The model is shown in Figure 1. It is important to note that the E3 Model proposes that the three phases may not be distinct from each other. Individuals targeted by relationship violence might move up and down along the y-axis, shifting temporarily from one phase to the next. Phases

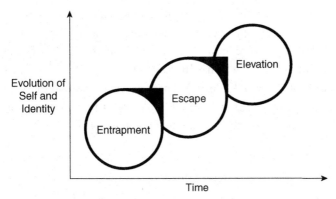

Note: As time progresses (x-axis), ideally the IPV target's evolution of self-concept, self-esteem, and identity will also progress (y-axis). The three phases are depicted as overlapping to emphasize that movement up and down along the y-axis is possible, although the overall trajectories are forward-moving for people who eventually reach Elevation.

Figure 1 The E3 Model of experiencing IPV

may also have significant overlap with each other. For example, targets of IPV will leave and return to an abuser an average of seven times before leaving permanently (NDVH, 2021), moving back and forth from the Entrapment and Escape phases. Someone might be psychologically ready to Escape, but pragmatic concerns keep them in Entrapment (for the time being). The psychological scaffolding needed to Escape might be built while someone is still in the relationship. In other words, the E3 Model is not a strict stage model; progressive growth over time might be delayed or convoluted by temporary backward motion. We use the word "phase" instead of "stage" to emphasize this point. The model is applicable to people who do eventually move through to the end, which is not the case for people who stay in their relationship or are killed by their abuser. We hope the model can offer help and optimism to those in need of it.

Phase 1, Entrapment, focuses on how people first enter into and become committed to a relationship that later becomes violent, and how experiencing IPV affects the self. Phase 2, Escape, explores how victims grow into survivors as they slowly build the resources needed to leave safely, including bolstering self-esteem. Finally, Phase 3, Elevation, centers on how survivors psychologically grow from their experience and become stronger, happier selves.

Note that terminology regarding people experiencing IPV can be controversial. Some scholars and activists believe that the word "victim" should never be used for those who are abused by their partners because it connotes "helplessness and pity" (Helloflo.com, 2021; see also Kirkwood, 1993; Romero-Sánchez et al., 2020). Many suggest that "survivor" is better because it connotes someone who has the strength to endure hardship and become empowered afterward. Throughout this Element, we approach the terminology from a scientific perspective in which "victim" will refer to someone who is still being abused, and "survivor" will refer to someone who has successfully escaped this violence. It is also important to note that the E3 Model is particularly relevant to forms of IPV in which one partner abuses the other – what social psychologists call intimate partner terrorism – as opposed to mutual or situational forms of IPV (Johnson, 1995, 2007).

2 Entrapment

The first phase of the E3 Model is *Entrapment*, the initial attraction to and formation of a relationship with a partner who will become abusive. Rosen (1996) first suggested the word "entrapment" when describing her own qualitative research with young women who were still in or had recently left abusive relationships. Her work sought how to best understand and empower them.

Rosen interviewed twenty-two women and identified several themes regarding how people still in violent relationships psychologically responded to IPV in ways that kept them committed despite the violence. Themes included (for example) "romantic fusion," in which the relationship becomes one's all-encompassing identity and passion, and "illusions of control," the unrealistic belief that things might change for the better if only the victim herself could find the key to changing the perpetrator's behavior. A third theme was "romantic fantasies," described in more detail in the Section 2.1.

In addition to Rosen's (1996) pioneering work, several other scholars have contributed theory and research regarding how experiencing relationship violence affects one's sense of self and perception of the relationship. Many studies provide evidence of the link between IPV and lowered self-esteem, as well as several other negative well-being outcomes (e.g., Choi, 2020; Pereira et al., 2020; Sáez et al., 2021). We highlight some of these important contributions to understanding the Entrapment phase later in the Element, focusing on work tied to perceptions of the self. Again, we exclude research on mutual forms of IPV and focus instead on work regarding intimate partner terrorism (Johnson, 1995, 2007).

2.1 Romantic Myths and Fantasies: Prescriptive Cultural Norms

One influence on the self-concept is culture. Culture can shape social norms, expectations of gender performance, goals, values, and so on. Cultural values are passed from one generation to the next through social agents such as parents, peers, and the media (Bandura, 1986). The stories children hear and see can change their expectations regarding roles within relationships and what is (or is not) appropriate behavior. In this way, women may be groomed by a culture preparing them to become Entrapped in future IPV before they even meet their partners – and men may be taught unhealthy gender roles and expectations from a toxic patriarchal perspective.

For example, male characters in children's picture books are significantly more likely to be portrayed outdoors and/or in paid professions, while girls and women are portrayed indoors and in nurturing roles such as caring for others (Hamilton et al., 2006). The subtle messages in such stories could imply that boys and men are active problem-solvers while girls and women should be more passive and subservient to others – prescriptive norms that affect heterosexual relationships (Prentice & Carranza, 2002). For example, when people endorse traditional gendered prescriptive norms, "women may act nurturant and warm on dates and men may act dominant and chivalrous" (Eagly et al., 2004, p. 275). These norms are taught via cultural messages and give permission for men to have traits such as aggression and dominance, which can take negative forms when used to control their partners.

Media aimed at children and adolescents may contribute to Entrapment into IPV relationships through what social psychologists label "romantic myths" (e.g., Cava et al., 2020; Masanet et al., 2018; Sánchez-Hernández et al., 2020). Romantic myths are unrealistic expectations perpetuated through cultural messages such as that love can overcome all difficulties, belief in love at first sight, or that love is associated with jealousy and possessiveness (Cava et al., 2020). Romantic myths may therefore emphasize prescriptive norms of male dominance by couching these expectations as "romantic." Men and women might internalize these norms as part of their identity. Self-discrepancy theory (Higgins, 1987) proposes that we all have three identities: our actual self (current self-concept), our ideal self (who we hope to become), and our ought self (the person we believe others want us to be). The ought self is affected by our understanding of prescriptive norms and cultural expectations of how we "should" act – and we are taught these lessons very early (Levinson & Rodebaugh, 2013).

As noted previously, Rosen (1996) identified examples of these cultural influences on relationships in her interviews with victims and survivors of IPV. Two specific romantic fantasies emerged that she linked to culture-based fairy tales taught to young children. The first is what she called the Cinderella fantasy (p. 159): "the illusion that a man can transform a woman's life, erase her insecurities, protect her from her fears, or save her from her problems." A key to the Cinderella fantasy is that young women are taught that a heterosexual male relationship partner is the path toward a better future, an idea especially appealing for women who struggle from low socioeconomic status or abusive families of origin, just like the original heroine of the story. Rosen notes that this fantasy is unrealistic and promotes dependency on a partner instead of empowering women to create their own happy endings. The same fantasy and negative gender-based outcomes have been called the "glass slipper effect" by other scholars (Rudman & Heppen, 2003).

Rosen's interviews also led to what she called the Beauty and the Beast fantasy (1996). Here, the fairy tale promotes the fantasy that women should be attracted to aggressive or troubled men who – with enough love and sacrifice from their partners – can be transformed into loving princes. This fantasy excuses "beastly" behavior as not the perpetrator's fault and instead can put the blame on the victim or survivor herself through the implication that she has simply not been patient or accommodating enough.

The notion of romantic fantasies or myths underlying unhealthy and/or abusive relationships has been supported by others. Jackson (2001) suggested that cultural romantic narratives (like fairy tales) teach that violent behavior from male partners is an expression of their love and that women should endure these challenges until their love magically transforms their partners. Another recent study found that romantic myths such as the beliefs that love is suffering, jealousy is a sign of love, and one must have a romantic partner to be happy are tied to accepting abusive behaviors, partially by not recognizing them as atypical or coercive (Cava et al., 2020). These myths are shown to affect both men and women in terms of their decreased likelihood of labeling problematic behaviors as abusive (Sánchez-Hernández et al., 2020). In sum, one way that identity and self-concept are affected by culture is by the messages young people are taught about what to expect from romantic relationships – and sometimes these myths and fantasies unknowingly promote unrealistic and unhealthy expectations and perceptions.

The E3 Model applies to all genders who are targets of IPV. Endorsement of myths about sexual aggression is significantly associated with victimization within relationships for men and women in heterosexual relationships, especially in cultures that value traditional gender norms (Fernández-Fuertes et al., 2020). This victimization disrupts self-determination and personal identity development (Parra-Barrera et al., 2021). Prescriptive norms about male dominance may also contribute to the minimization of men's experience when they are the targets of IPV; they are sometimes not taken as seriously as women who report the same events (Arnocky & Vaillancourt, 2014; Machado et al., 2017). Much more research is needed regarding men and nonbinary people who are victims.

2.2 Invisible Impacts on the Self: Sexual and Emotional Violence

Once people have formed adult intimate relationships, different forms of IPV may affect the self in different ways. One of the most traumatic forms of IPV may be sexual violence, which is estimated to occur in about 10 percent of intimate relationships (McLindon et al., 2018). Sexual violence can disrupt one's sense of self and lead to psychological scars, including lowered self-esteem and other negative mental health outcomes (Roth & Lebowitz, 1988). It is tied to Entrapment because sexual behaviors can lead one to feel more emotionally invested in a partner and therefore less likely to leave despite low satisfaction overall (Rusbult & Martz, 1995).

One study that focused on sexual violations within intimate relationships summarized the experience of these invisible impacts as "being attacked from the inside out" (Tarzia, 2021a). In-depth interviews with women in Australia revealed four themes in terms of how IPV (specifically sexual IPV in this study) can affect one's sense of self. "Shaken foundations" is a feeling of personal confusion and betrayal regarding perceptions of one's place in the relationship. "A different kind of damage" is feelings of shame, guilt, and self-blame that many victims experienced, as well as an overarching sense of lost control over one's life. "Lingering scar tissue" refers to a shaken self-concept, including a pervasive sense of vulnerability to others, doubting one's personal social judgments, and loss of interest in sexual behaviors. The final theme identified in this research was called "it kills something inside you." This theme centered around a dazed self-concept and self-esteem. Victims of sexual IPV describe struggling with body image, confidence, and self-esteem in response to dehumanizing behavior from their partners. These negative effects can be aggravated when one's culture endorses the idea that sex is a "woman's duty" in heterosexual relationships, another example of prescriptive norms (Tarzia, 2021b).

In addition to physical and sexual abuse, emotional and/or psychological abuse can be particularly damaging to one's self-concept and self-esteem. Perpetrators of IPV purposely use power and control tactics to keep their victims subdued; these tactics include shifting the blame to the victim, minimizing the perceived effects of emotional aggression, economic control, isolating the victim, threats, and more (Pence & Paymar, 1993; Ubillos-Landa et al., 2020). Over time, being subjected to these tactics undermines and erodes victims' self-esteem.

Research from Kirkwood (1993) concentrates on how emotional IPV affects identity. Using unstructured interviews with women who eventually left their abusers, she identifies six ways in which victims respond to emotional abuse in terms of psychological perceptions and the self. First is degradation, when victims perceive they are less valued and socially acceptable than most other people. This devaluing of the self can result from a perpetrator's repeated criticism and insults. The second response is fear; victims perceive that the world is unpredictable, which causes anxiety and a pervasive sense of danger. Victims' locus of control moves from internal (the belief they determine their own fate) to external (the belief that their future is in the hands of another; Rotter, 1966, 1975). Third, victims of emotional IPV perceive that their bodies are viewed as sexual objects to be used by their abuser or by others in general. This objectification is tied to victims losing a healthy self-concept that includes "inner energy, resources, needs, [and] desires" (Kirkwood, 1993, pp. 50–51). Other research supports the idea that when victims of IPV feel sexually objectified, they are more likely to silence their needs and feel a lost sense of self (Sáez et al., 2020).

The fourth result of emotional IPV, according to Kirkwood (1993), is deprivation. Victims perceive an almost constant lack of their needs being met, such as economic, safety, and social needs. This deprivation is associated with a self-concept in which one accepts (at least, temporarily) intense isolation and gives up relationships with friends, family, or community social roles. Fifth, Kirkwood notes that victims' self-concept will change to include an overburden of responsibility. This is experienced as an overwhelming sense of exhaustion and sacrifice needed to maintain the relationship and household. One's identity now incorporates the roles of family manager, housekeeper, and (at least in some relationships) assistant or servant to the perpetrator.

Finally, Kirkwood's (1993) research suggests that emotional IPV is tied to a distortion of subjective reality in the victims' perceptions. A component of this sixth result may be a ubiquitous sense of terror and doubt. This fear may be the result of what some researchers call gaslighting when a perpetrator acts in ways designed to make their victim feel "crazy" or doubt their memories and perceptions (Knapp, 2019; Sweet, 2019). It may also include extremely low self-esteem and potentially a lack of any stable self-concept at all – what Kirkwood described as a "sickening caricature of what [the victims] once believed" about themselves and their world (1993, p. 57).

2.3 Cognitive Reframing and Dissonance

Other research from social psychology has explored how experiencing IPV can lead to a cognitive reframing of the self-concept (e.g., Arriaga, 2002; Goodfriend & Arriaga, 2018). Being victimized, manipulated, or abused by one's partner goes against culturally expected schemas of relationships. In addition, most people do not want to think of themselves as "victims" or as someone who would "put up with" this kind of abuse from a partner. So, when IPV occurs, one possible outcome is for the victim to reframe either the situation or their sense of self to resolve this sense of dissonance (Festinger & Carlsmith, 1959).

Victims of IPV may cognitively reframe the abusive behaviors by minimizing their severity or by interpreting them as not counting as abuse or violence. A notable example is a quantitative study with a community sample of middle-aged women that found victims of severe behaviors (such as being kicked or burned by their partners) sometimes interpreted these actions as "just joking around" or teasing that had accidentally gone too far (Arriaga, 2002). This interpretation was more likely in victims who were highly committed to staying with their partners. Another study using interviews of women in a shelter found that victims who were not able to leave their relationship coped with the dissonance of staying with an abuser by redefining the definition of "abuse" (Goodfriend & Arriaga, 2018). Here, some victims explained that their partners were not abusers because, although he used physical, sexual, or emotional aggression, it was not "abuse" as it did not cause lasting physical injury or was not done with a closed fist.

Similar coping strategies may, unfortunately, lead victims to blame themselves instead of their partners (Campbell et al., 2009). Here, the victim's self-concept and self-esteem have been manipulated by the partner until they internalize shame and guilt for the IPV. Interviews revealed self-blame as a pervasive effect of IPV in one study when women were asked to describe a particularly violent incident in their relationship and what caused it to occur (Goodfriend & Arriaga, 2018). Participants responded with statements such as "I am partly to blame for all this," "Maybe I pushed his buttons," and "There must be something that I'm doing wrong if he's hitting me or beating me up" (p. 5). Changing one's self-concept to include blame for being victimized – and the lowered self-esteem that accompanies that change – is a heartbreaking aspect of IPV.

Cognitive dissonance theory (Festinger & Carlsmith, 1959) asserts that when people have incompatible thoughts and/or behaviors (e.g., I believe relationship abuse is unacceptable; I am being abused by my partner), one solution is to change one of the thoughts or behaviors to avoid the anxiety produced. People might reframe the behaviors so they no longer count as violent or they might justify staying by switching the blame from the perpetrator to the self. While cognitive dissonance may explain reframing and self-blame, there are other valid theoretical explanations for these phenomena.

A possible alternative to cognitive dissonance is learned helplessness (Maier & Seligman, 1976; Seligman, 1972). This theory suggests that when people are exposed to prolonged negative events outside of their control, their motivation, emotions, and sense of self are compromised. This includes a shift in their locus of control from internal to external, resulting in feelings of helplessness that can generalize to their overall sense of self, not just specifically relevant to the causal situation or relationship. Effects on victims of violence can be "emotional numbness," "maladaptive passivity," and lowered general self-esteem (Peterson & Seligman, 1983). Learned helplessness may be one explanation for why survivors of one abusive relationship enter others; they perceive a loss of ability to change their situation, their partners, or the culture that produces such behaviors (Follingstad et al., 1988).

All theoretical explanations converge on the replicated finding that being victimized by IPV is associated with a vulnerable self-concept, decreased self-esteem, and fractured overall identity. This state is likely one reason why many victims find it so difficult to leave their partners, moving from the phase of

Entrapment to Escape. Many current victims also experience what social psychology calls a lack of affective forecasting – the inability to predict how we will feel in the future (Buehler & McFarland, 2001; Gilbert et al., 1998; Hoerger et al., 2010). A longitudinal, quantitative study first asked IPV victims to predict how happy they might be if their relationship ended (Arriaga et al., 2013). Several months later, follow-up surveys found that about one-quarter of the participants had successfully Escaped, and the survivors were significantly happier than they had predicted. While the Escape process is daunting, many people do eventually leave. On average, an IPV victim will leave and return to an abusive relationship seven times before leaving permanently (NDVH, 2021), emphasizing the overlap between the Entrapment and Escape phases of the E3 Model.

In sum, Entrapment – the first phase in the E3 Model – suggests that experiencing IPV has many and varied effects on one's self-concept, self-esteem, and identity. Cultural influences such as romantic myths and prescriptive norms influence expectations and ideas of how we "ought" to act in relationships; these influences can result in negative outcomes when one partner abuses another. These negative effects may be particularly likely when sexual and emotional abuse occurs, which can lead to confusion and cognitive reframing of the self. Entrapment, or getting into an abusive relationship, creates barriers to leaving – but some people do successfully Escape.

3 Escape

Moving from Entrapment to Escape – the second phase in the E3 Model – is difficult. *Escape* refers to successfully leaving an abusive relationship permanently (although ties to the abuser may still need to exist for pragmatic reasons such as child custody). Many people will phase back and forth between Entrapment, Escape, and Elevation as they attempt to leave and fail; leave temporarily and go back; and psychologically struggle with their identity along the way. Successful Escape requires salient pragmatic and immediate needs such as adequate housing, medical aid, and protection from the former perpetrator (Kirkwood, 1993). Leaving a partner might mean loss of financial stability as well, a strong mediator between the degree of abuse and well-being after Escape (Sauber & O'Brien, 2020). Psychological and emotional needs are more varied and potentially much longer-lasting. A primary psychological need in the Escape phase of the E3 Model is nurturing and rebuilding identity and self-esteem.

Kirkwood (1993) describes how survivors in the acute phase immediately after ending a relationship experience rapidly shifting priorities and reactions including a deep sense of relief, grief for their lost relationship, and missing their partners (despite acknowledging the abuse). Numbness and shock often follow, which are eventually replaced with a deep sense of achievement. Lost internal locus of control is slowly regained as the balance of power shifts from the ex-partner to the survivor. This evolution of one's self-concept and self-esteem are also explored by other researchers, each of whom highlights a different important aspect of Escape.

3.1 Self-Reclaiming Actions: Rebuilding Self-Esteem

Lowered self-esteem is a ubiquitous result of IPV (Giles-Sims, 1998; Walker, 1984). How do victims and survivors reclaim lost confidence and rebuild an integrated, empowered self-concept? Rosen explored the steps survivors must take to achieve these outcomes (Rosen & Stith, 1997). She refers to a process of "self-reclaiming actions" (p. 177), strides toward an emboldened self. These steps can take different forms.

Sometimes self-reclaiming actions are in the form of taking control as a step toward leaving the relationship (Rosen & Stith, 1997). Victims may begin to set boundaries for what is and is not acceptable. This may also include the realization that while one is not responsible for the abuse coming from their partners, they are responsible for the actions needed to Escape. This requires embracing an internal locus of control. Importantly, victims must form a meta-awareness of themselves and their situation, including the eventual realization that they are, in fact, victims of IPV and that they do not deserve their partners' abusive treatments. Both their self-esteem and self-concept must therefore become galvanized in order to shift from victims to survivors when they find the strength to Escape, restore personal agency, and rebuild their lives.

Part of reclaiming the self is exploring how one's identity is no longer "enmeshed" with the former abuser (Rusbult & Martz, 1995). During Entrapment, "the partner is no longer experienced as a distinct individual deserving of respect but instead, as an extension of [the abuser's] self" (Sabourin, 1995, p. 281). The victim's identity is subjugated during Entrapment and must be reconstructed after Escape (Olson, 2004). One scholar notes that this reconstruction must involve an inner voice free of judgment from others and free from an ex-partner's influence. This process is further elucidated next.

3.2 Unraveling the Self: Establishing Psychological Independence

As briefly mentioned earlier, several social psychological theories explore how one's sense of self can overlap with and encompass one's partner, especially in highly committed relationships (e.g., self-expansion theory [Aron & Aron, 1986], interdependence theory [Kelley & Thibaut, 1978], and cognitive interdependence theory [Agnew et al., 1998]). This bonding may be especially acute in partners with insecure attachment (see Clulow, 2012; Costa & Botelheiro, 2021; Dutton et al., 1994). "Malignant bonding" refers to the severe emotional deprivation often found in victims of IPV and the resultant need for approval from their abuser (Welldon, 2011; see also Dutton & Painter, 1981). When such attachment and bonding exist, Escape becomes especially difficult.

The ability to psychologically unravel one's self-concept from an abusive partner is relevant to this phase of the E3 Model. One study interviewed women in France and focused on how this process may occur in survivors; these researchers identified four themes (Metz et al., 2019). The first was "a new life and increased awareness." This theme centered on survivors' need to irrevocably break the tie to their partners in their self-concept. Subthemes were (a) blaming the ex-partner for the violence and not the self, (b) the need to be recognized as an independent person not tied to the partner, (c) unresolved childhood issues in their ex-partner and/or self, (d) acknowledging that leaving would not resolve all their difficulties immediately, (e) haunting traumatic memories, and (f) the importance of therapy to help rebuild their lives, self-concept, and self-esteem.

Three other themes emerged from this study (Metz et al., 2019). One was the survivors' description of how relationships with family and friends were further complicated by leaving their partners. Sometimes, this was because of a lack of support for ending the relationship, what other researchers have called "family collusion" (Rosen, 1996). A second theme was that survivors' daily experiences now included fear and the possibility of violence (even after Escape, fear remains). Finally, survivors noted that an essential part of Escape was finding a way out. This final phase included understanding laws and criminal justice resources available to them as well as acknowledging what is (and is not) realistic. The final phase included a personal analysis of how their fragile self-concept may have been affected by childhood experiences as well as by their abusive partner. The authors of this study note that each step may be needed to help people Escape the trap their abuser has put them in.

3.3 Rebuilding a Fractured Identity: Confronting the Experience

Social psychology underscores that our identities are part of a larger social context. Specifically, social identity theory suggests that our self-concept is made up of both personal factors (such as skills or personality traits) and social roles and relationships (Sherif, 1966; Tajfel, 1981, 1982). The larger cultural environment affects both aspects through structures like gender norms, structural prejudice, and socially accepted values – including the idea that violence is sometimes appropriate (Liang et al., 2005).

Brewer's (2001) extended version of social identity theory delineates four specific parts of our social self-concept: a person-based social identity (e.g., gender and ethnicity), relational identity (including family and intimate relationships), group-based identity (such as chosen social groups or team memberships), and collective identity (larger social roles in which we belong such as "mothers" or "wives"). While these identities shift over any person's lifetime, they can also conflict with each other or be shaped by outside forces. Experiencing IPV may be one force that threatens our self-concept and current identity, including our self-esteem and each part of our social self-concept (Hague et al., 2003; Moss et al., 1997).

O'Doherty et al. (2016) explored how IPV specifically affects the four aspects of identity laid out in Brewer's (2001) framework. They hypothesized that perpetrators of IPV would undermine person-based identity by attacking their victims' very concept of self through emphasizing a sense of failure. Perpetrators might also attack relational and group-based identities by isolating victims, negatively comparing them to others, and violating their attachments to others. Finally, the research team expected that perpetrators may undercut and destabilize their victims' collective identity by replacing any previously held roles with only that of serving the abusers' needs. In short, they suggested that from a social identity theory perspective, IPV replaces one's healthy and independent identity with a distorted and dysfunctional "abuse identity" (p. 234). Once the abuse identity is present, it is difficult to Escape.

They interviewed survivors in Australia and found evidence that IPV does affect each of these aspects of self-concept (O'Doherty et al., 2016). One participant noted, "It was that experience . . . where I couldn't recognize myself in the mirror, when I just said this is wrong" (p. 231). Perpetrators controlled what their victims were and weren't allowed to do, therefore pulling the strings of social relationships, roles, and expectations. An example of this control was expressed by a participant who said, "you don't feel like you can be a mother anymore. You think you're so beyond it that you're not worthy of that role" (p. 232). These manipulated and fluctuating identities were summed up by a third participant who expressed, "I didn't have an identity of my own. Yeah, I didn't have my own life, like I was his possession" (p. 232).

How are these fractured identities rebuilt in the Escape phase? The same study (O'Doherty et al., 2016) outlined ways that survivors can reconstruct self-concept and self-esteem after leaving their partners. Sometimes, they also had to get a divorce to Escape their abuser. When this happens in cultures largely disapproving of divorce, it can mean struggling between one's person-based identity (individuality and safety) versus their group-based or collective identity (e.g., Akangbe Tomisin, 2020). Next, their participants reported initially concealing their history of abuse as a way to preserve their public identity and sense of self beyond the relationship. This concealment temporarily allowed them to avoid stigma and re-traumatization, providing space for reflection and healing. Eventually, concealment of past or present IPV had to end so that opportunities to Escape and/or heal could occur.

Survivors explicitly noted the value of rebuilding their self-esteem and gaining new social identities (O'Doherty et al., 2016). Interestingly, survivors explained that eventually, their originally fractured identities had led to help-seeking. To move from victim to survivor, they had to confront their situation and priorities and find the motivation to change things. Supportive interactions with social workers and health care providers sometimes created a path to Escape. Throughout the entire process from Entrapment to Escape, identity is in flux as survivors navigate where they fit in a social world that may not empathize or understand. As one survivor put it, "I constantly feel like I'm still trying to move away from that whole [experience] . . . . I'm in that category of something that they'll still never understand" (p. 240). Male survivors of IPV may especially struggle with finding social support, as many cultures are much less understanding and empathetic to their experience (Arnocky & Vaillancourt, 2014). A cultural assumption of male dominance may increase the stigma and embarrassment men feel when attempting to leave female abusers, leading them to be significantly less likely to report the violence or seek help (Allen-Collinson, 2009).

3.4 Embracing a New Self: Preparing for Elevation

Envisioning a better future and embracing a new self are vital to survivors' health and happiness. Survival and coping tactics that worked well previously – such as minimizing the situation, numbing emotions, or isolation – may now be detrimental to forging a new, stronger self-concept and self-esteem. An example of this cognitive shift from one survivor's story is: "I felt like a victim for a long while but now I'm in control of my own life . . . . I'm healthier today, and I'm happier, feel a lot better about myself" (Kirkwood, 1993, p. 136).

As Escape begins to overlap with Elevation, survival tactics shift to those that will help the transition. Kirkwood's (1993) analysis provides several dimensions of change. The first is "addressing, exploring and fulfilling one's own needs" (p. 139). A transformation is needed in which survivors shift from living for the needs of their abuser to instead focusing on what they, themselves, want and need. Personal needs may have been sacrificed for years, so part of this journey is deciding what preferences and goals exist in their own, empowered self-concept. In Kirkwood's research, one-fifth of survivors went back to school to complete degrees, while others explored musical talents or experimented with fashion choices. Some simply enjoy the freedom to do simple things like taking long baths. Survivors noted that surrounding themselves with friends and family who were supportive of this identity exploration was vital to success, as were caring and well-trained counseling services.

The second dimension of change at the end of Escape is "asserting the self and personal needs," especially in relationships with others (Kirkwood, 1993, p. 141). Importantly, many survivors are hesitant to start new intimate relationships – a pattern replicated by other work (e.g., Ko & Park, 2020; St. Vil et al., 2021). Survivors have to establish boundaries and learn how to assert themselves with others in ways that are comfortable and feel safe. Specifically, many of them create routines with built-in solitary time for journaling, exercise, or reflection. They are also more vocal about behaviors from their previous partner(s) they find troubling or triggering. Perhaps, most importantly, many survivors communicate more explicitly about their desire for a nonviolent and nonaggressive relationship dynamic with a new person.

Kirkwood's (1993) third dimension of embracing a new self during the final parts of what we call Escape is "effecting change" (p. 145). Here, many survivors feel the need to use their own experience within a larger community to help prevent or end IPV in others' relationships. While not all survivors become community activists, those who do can feel increased confidence and self-esteem. This process is often part of the overlap and transition between the Escape and Elevation phases and is discussed further below.

In sum, the Escape phase of the E3 Model focuses on the psychological needs of people who are starting to consider leaving and/or have left abusers, both immediately and long term. First, survivors will likely have to reclaim an independent identity that is no longer enmeshed with their partners. Next, they will rebuild self-esteem and explore a new identity with new opportunities. These transitions are buttressed by supportive friends, family, and communities. Many people in the overlap between Escape and Elevation will be motivated by activism to prevent IPV and help other victims and survivors. This emphasis on justice and social change is explored in more detail in the last phase of our framework.

4 Elevation

What lies beyond the pain of IPV victimization and the struggle that survivors of such violence face to rebuild self-concept and self-esteem? When survivors do successfully leave their abusers, healing and reconstruction of the self may be difficult (Giles-Sims, 1998). However, several promising areas of research suggest that this difficulty may be overcome to complete the third phase proposed in the E3 Model: Elevation. *Elevation* in this model is defined as the evolution of identity and self-esteem in the aftermath of IPV in which people transcend their experiences by becoming stronger and happier selves.

One of the primary ways that current literature describes the various types of what we label Elevation following IPV is through the theory of post-traumatic growth (PTG; D'Amore et al., 2018; Street & Arias, 2001; Tedeschi & Calhoun, 1996). This form of growth includes key changes to a survivor's outlook on life and self, including the development of closer, more intimate, and more meaningful relationships with others; an improved sense of personal strength; greater appreciation for life in general; spiritual growth; and an optimistic recognition of new possibilities for one's life (Tedeschi & Calhoun, 2004a). PTG theory describes particular ways that IPV survivors may experience Elevation. It is important to note, however, that the changes the theory identifies are not the only ways that individuals experience Elevation. There are potentially as many unique experiences of Elevation as there are survivors of IPV. We describe work on PTG in more detail below.

Next, this Element focuses on two potential mechanisms to achieve and express the Elevation phase of the E3 Model: storytelling and service to others. Many people who have experienced IPV want to tell and share their stories. Sharing the experience of trauma provides survivors with a sense of closure and with an improved self-concept (Pennebaker, 1997; Sharma-Patel et al., 2012). Elevated self-concept and self-esteem may also arise as a result of working to support other victims of IPV and through efforts for justice and social change in the community and larger culture.

4.1 Elevating Identity through Struggle: Post-Traumatic Growth

The negative consequences of IPV, including physical injury and psychological injuries such as depression, post-traumatic stress disorder, anxiety, suicidal ideation and attempts, and substance abuse/dependence, have been well documented in the psychological literature (Basile et al., 2004; Beydoun et al., 2012; Devries et al., 2013; Dillon et al., 2013; Macy et al., 2009; Nathanson et al., 2012). More recently, a growing body of research has sought to understand how and why IPV survivors experience positive changes following traumatic experiences in the context of IPV (Bakaityte et al., 2020; Brosi et al., 2020; D'Amore et al., 2018; Valdez & Lilly, 2015; Wood, 2017). Researchers have referred to the positive changes that survivors experience in different ways including "stress-related growth," "benefit-finding," and "PTG" (Helgeson et al., 2006). This Element will focus specifically on the latter (PTG).

The concept of PTG grew out of the field of positive psychology in an attempt to understand how people grow and change positively following adversity (Seligman & Csikszentmihalyi, 2000). The actual term "post-traumatic growth" was coined by Tedeschi and Calhoun (1996, 2004a, 2004b) to describe the significant positive psychological growth that follows an individual's struggle with trauma, growth that surpasses levels of psychological functioning prior to the traumatic experience (Calhoun & Tedeschi, 1998; Tedeschi & Calhoun, 2004a).

The word "struggle" is a critical aspect of PTG that may explain why IPV survivors have the potential to Elevate their self-concept and self-esteem following periods of Entrapment and Escape. Tedeschi and Calhoun propose that it is not an adverse or traumatic event itself that triggers PTG, but rather the "struggle with the new reality" following the trauma (Tedeschi & Calhoun, 2004a, p. 5). It is important to make a clear distinction that the survivor is not "better off" for having experienced IPV, but rather has experienced positive outcomes because of their individual efforts to overcome the trauma they experienced (D'Amore et al., 2018; Tedeschi & Calhoun, 2004a).

There is a discrepancy in the literature regarding the timing of PTG in relation to IPV, specifically whether the growth may occur while a survivor is still involved in an abusive relationship or the growth occurs only after the survivor Escapes. A study by Cobb et al. (2006) supported Tedeschi and Calhoun's (1995) theory that the majority of PTG occurs after the survivor Escapes. However, that same study cautioned that a survivor who is still trapped in an abusive relationship may experience growth during periods when they are temporarily away from the abusive partner and also during periods when the survivor is still experiencing IPV after leaving the relationship (e.g., when forced to interact with the abuser during custody issues). In summary, while most PTG occurs after Escape, it is possible to experience PTG while simultaneously experiencing IPV. This aspect of PTG reinforces the theory posited by the E3 Model that the three phases are not strictly distinct from one another and that progression through the phases may not be linear.

Regardless of whether PTG occurs while a survivor is still Entrapped or following Escape, three general areas of PTG may change as a result of struggling with the experience (Tedeschi & Calhoun, 1995): perception of self, experiences of relationships with others, and outlook on life. The researchers later (Tedeschi & Calhoun, 1996, 2004a) utilized factor analysis to further identify five domains that may elucidate how PTG affects a survivor's identity: (1) greater appreciation of life, (2) more intimate relationships with others, (3) greater sense of personal strength, (4) recognition of new possibilities in life, and (5) spiritual development.

There is a growing body of research on PTG from traumas that are similar to IPV or that directly investigate trauma associated with IPV. A systematic review of sixteen studies that evaluated PTG in adult survivors of interpersonal violence (Elderton et al., 2017) included studies that specifically focused on IPV (Cobb et al., 2006; Hou et al., 2013; Senter & Caldwell, 2002; Song, 2012; Taylor, 2004). Reviewers concluded that the mean prevalence of PTG in interpersonal violence survivors was around 71 percent (with a range from 58 percent to 99 percent). The review reported that survivors described growth in all five PTG domains, with the "appreciation of life" and "personal strength" domains showing the highest levels of survivor growth. These findings demonstrated a higher level of survivor PTG than an earlier review (Linley & Joseph, 2004), which reported survivor growth rates of 30–70 percent following exposure to a variety of traumatic events. The significant prevalence rates identified in the Elderton et al. (2017) review indicate that the concept of PTG is relevant to understanding how and why IPV survivors Elevate their self-concepts following exposure to IPV.

Other literature that specifically links IPV to growth explores this relevance. An empirical review (Ulloa et al., 2015) concluded that IPV survivors consistently demonstrate psychological growth following experiences with violent relationships and linked the identified growth to the three general PTG categories labeled perception of self, experiences of relationships with others, and outlook on life. Valdez and Lilly (2015) also explored the relationship between PTG and IPV survivors. This longitudinal study evaluated the relationship between PTG and Janoff-Bulman's (1992, 2006) model of world assumptions as they relate to PTG. Researchers evaluated schema reconstruction for women following IPV. Survivors were evaluated at two points, baseline and approximately one year later. Findings revealed that 87 percent of the survivors reported PTG over the one-year period of the study, regardless of whether or not they had been revictimized. The survivors who were able to positively reconstruct their schema of the world within the study period experienced the highest levels of PTG. Similar findings were reported by D'Amore et al. (2018) during their secondary analysis of survivor narratives. Evidence of PTG was reported in the "Renewal and Reconstruction" theme that emerged during analysis as the survivors discussed changes in their sense of self and in their relationships. Similar evidence emerged in the "Transformation and Meaning" theme as survivors described the happiness and contentment they found following their experiences with IPV along with pride, forgiveness, gratitude, and hope. Though this study did not specifically evaluate survivors of PTG, the narratives that were analyzed clearly displayed elements of the PTG domains.

Other work has utilized IPV survivor narratives to examine the pathways that survivors use to move toward PTG (Brosi et al., 2020). The study examined survivor narratives of escape from an abusive relationship and analyzed these stories to determine the factors that provided opportunities for PTG. Findings showed that the survivor narratives incorporated multiple PTG domains of growth, including changes in life perspective, self-perception, interpersonal relationships, and spiritual growth. Findings further revealed four primary themes that related directly to the PTG domains: (1) deliberateness of action, described as a survivor's changed beliefs about their situation and the determination to act on those beliefs; (2) motivation to end the cycle of violence for their children; (3) changed perspective on life, specifically those perspectives that involve self-sufficiency, power to create positive change, and the right to have healthy relationships that are free of violence; and (4) alternative perceptions of social support that include family, friends, shelters, and faith-based communities. This study's emphasis on the value of social support is important and is addressed further in the next section of this Element.

While the previously cited studies establish a clear link between IPV and PTG, how this link specifically supports the Elevation of identity, and corresponding self-concept and self-esteem, was not addressed. This link was explored by another team of researchers (Bakaityte et al., 2020). Their longitudinal study included a significant survivor sample size, encompassing 217 women who had experienced IPV. Results indicated that higher levels of PTG at the beginning of the two-year study were positively associated with identity exploration. Higher levels of PTG were correlated with the likelihood that survivors perceived their IPV experiences as central to their identity and with an exploration of possible identity choices. The study discussed how IPV experiences may shatter survivors' identities, which raises the opportunity for new identities to arise. The co-occurring processes of identity exploration and PTG could happen simultaneously when the survivors' core beliefs about themselves are challenged following an experience of IPV (Jenks, 2014). The study found that identity-related PTG did not change longitudinally over the course of the study itself, pointing toward the hypothesis that PTG is most likely to occur in the years immediately after Escape.

Taken together, the studies cited provide evidence that many IPV survivors experience PTG in the aftermath of trauma, that the domains of PTG point toward positive changes in self-concept and self-esteem, and finally that identity exploration in IPV survivors may correlate with PTG. Note an important caveat:

PTG is more fluctuating and dynamic than the slow process of identity formation over an entire lifetime (Tedeschi et al., 2018).

PTG research offers invaluable insights into how an extremely negative experience, such as IPV, may help change and forge anew a trauma survivor's identity in such a way that the survivor experiences Elevation as defined in the E3 Model. The post-traumatic growth inventory scale (Tedeschi & Calhoun, 1996) identifies twenty-five important changes that may have occurred in an IPV survivor's life as a result of the trauma they experienced, grouped into five factors. These changes, while certainly descriptive of the Elevation phase, are not the only way that survivors' self-concepts and self-esteem can change in positive ways. Other changes are described in the survivors' own words through the process of telling their stories.

4.2 Rebuilding Self-Concept through Story: Healing Narratives

The ability to psychologically unravel one's self-concept from a former abuser is a critical aspect of both Escaping from an abusive relationship and of rebuilding a fractured identity. One of the ways survivors may support themselves in this rebuilding process is by creating a narrative for their lives that is independent of the abuser and that frames their IPV experience in such a way that self-concept is supported and Elevated. Such narratives have been shown to demonstrate positive outcomes for IPV survivors (Moreira et al., 2020; Orang et al., 2018; Volpe et al., 2017). D'Amore et al. (2018) applied narrative thematic analysis (Braun & Clarke, 2006) to an existing data set (Hendrika et al., 2012; Tutty et al., 2009) to explore the positive outcomes survivors described through their narratives of IPV experiences. The research team examined the narratives of ten women who self-selected to participate in open-ended interviews.

Three major themes were identified in the women's storytelling, each of which related to the survivors' self-concept and to their social relationships (D'Amore et al., 2018). The first theme, "Awareness and Insight," highlighted how survivor experiences with IPV influenced identity. Within this theme, the process of "discerning the self" described survivor recognition of how the sense of self was initially eroded in the violent relationship and then later rebuilt by utilizing coping strategies (talking about the violence, participating in cultural and spiritual traditions, and attending counseling) to create a new sense of wholeness in their identities. Additional awareness and insight within this theme came through the process of newly understanding the relationship. This reflection and analysis facilitated the survivors' insight into how their abusive partners' controlling behavior affected them and their other family members (including children). Such understanding also highlighted deeper patterns of violence in the survivors' lives, helping them connect the former partners' controlling behavior to their own family-of-origin history and dynamics.

The second theme identified in the narratives, "Renewal and Reconstruction," addressed the survivors' processes of rebuilding their self-concept and of redefining relationships (D'Amore et al., 2018). The narratives directly described how the survivors viewed themselves following their experiences with IPV, thus indicating that the process of rebuilding the self is perhaps most closely linked to changes in self-concept. These positive changes included increased assertiveness skills, stronger personal boundaries, and greatly increased perceptions of personal power. One survivor vividly described her rebuilt and reconstructed self (p. 12):

> I got thinking, if I was seven feet tall with a whole bunch of muscles I could just pick him up . . . . And there came a day when I had support from the police and those counsellors and my minister that I said, "you know, for the first time in my life I am seven feet tall. Take your hands off me."

The overwhelming majority of survivors directly discussed positive changes in their self-concept and identity, writing explicitly about the selves that were "lost" to them when they experienced IPV and the new selves they rebuilt, selves that the research team described as "totally new to them" (p. 12). This positive process of renewal and rebuilding extended to the survivors' relationships with children, family, friends, current romantic partners, and their communities.

The third theme identified in the narratives, "Transformation and Meaning," described how survivors had developed "new perspectives" on their selves that directly relate to self-concept (D'Amore et al., 2018). Survivor narratives described feelings of happiness, contentment, and pride in what they had accomplished following their experiences with IPV. The narratives also described how survivors had developed new goals and a clear sense of hope for the future, both for themselves and for their children.

The positive changes in self-concept that were identified and thematically categorized by D'Amore et al. (2018) were inductively and deductively determined from narrative transcripts. While this secondary analysis had the advantage of providing distance from the direct data collection process in order to facilitate unbiased analysis, the process did not allow the researchers to engage in dialogue with the survivors, to ask clarifying questions, or to follow up on significant issues or themes that emerged during the process of storytelling. Recent research that documents positive storytelling outcomes for IPV survivors overcomes these limitations by focusing on storytelling in more interactive, therapeutic settings (Moreira et al., 2020; Orang et al., 2018; Volpe et al., 2017).

The storytelling method that is used most often in these settings, narrative exposure therapy (NET), is an evidence-based, short-term therapeutic tool originally designed to address survivor trauma associated with war and torture (Schauer et al., 2011). The therapeutic process of NET requires an individual to construct a chronological and coherent narrative of their life story with a particular focus on the traumatic experiences. The process, which is therapist-assisted, occurs over a predefined number of therapy sessions, typically four to twelve sessions that last approximately ninety minutes each (Elbert et al., 2015). NET has evolved as a therapeutic tool for survivors of IPV primarily because it focuses on a series of traumatic events rather than on a single event, a method that is ideally suited to the dynamics of IPV (Foa, 2011; Schauer et al., 2011). The body of research on NET with survivors of IPV is limited and focuses more directly on clinical symptomology than identity or self-concept. However, recent studies indicate that storytelling produces positive outcomes for IPV survivors as part of their Elevation process.

One example qualitative study (Volpe et al., 2017) focused on pregnant and parenting adolescents who had experienced high rates of IPV. The study explored the benefits of offering NET to IPV-exposed adolescents and concluded that both the survivors who received NET and the community-based service providers who provided the narrative therapy agreed that NET improves negative IPV-related mental health disorders.

A second study (Orang et al., 2018) investigated the efficacy of NET in a group of Iranian women who were currently living in violent relationships. The study compared NET outcomes to those derived from commonly used counseling methods for victims of IPV in Iran. Researchers concluded that primary outcome measures and reduction of trauma-related symptoms were positive for the victims who engaged in NET. The positive benefits were maintained longitudinally at the six-month follow-up. Positive results from these two NET studies led to a third study to investigate the effect of narrative therapy on survivors of IPV who have successfully Escaped (Moreira et al., 2020). This study utilized a different form of narrative therapy, cognitive-narrative therapy (CNT). This form of storytelling involves a deconstruction of the trauma narrative followed by the reconstruction of a new narrative that emphasizes multiple meanings and coherences (Gonçalves & Machado, 1999; Moreira et al., 2020). CNT emphasizes the power of the survivor as the "builder" of their experiences (Gonçalves, 2002; Moreira et al., 2020), emphasizing personal agency and an empowered self-concept that promote Elevation.

CNT has been further adapted for survivors of IPV (Moreira et al., 2020). Survivors attended four weekly sessions in this study. The first session, "Recalling," was designed to guide the survivors through the history of the violent relationship and into a specific and detailed IPV-related episode. The second session, "Emotional and Cognitive Subjectivation," sought to empower the survivors with a sense of authorship by guiding them through a narration of the feelings and thoughts associated with the recalled event from the first session. The therapist guides the survivors in making associations between feelings and thoughts. The third session, "Metaphorisation," guides them into creating a unifying metaphor (e.g., "ripping the sheet") that separates the previously described violent episode from the beginning of a new life that is free of violence. Finally, the fourth session, "Projection," encourages them to find a more positive metaphor for the episode, one that indicates a new chapter in their life.

Findings documented positive outcomes in mental health symptoms associated with IPV-related trauma for most survivors (Moreira et al., 2020). Though the study did not seek to specifically measure how storytelling influences self-concept, results still revealed statistically significant outcomes that were directly relevant. Survivors noted that the storytelling process was important to them because it helped them better organize their feelings, thoughts, and doubts; have less fear in connecting to others; and supported them in creating meaning for the IPV-related violence they experienced.

The Moreira et al. (2020) team noted that the narrative therapy process did produce a negative self-concept effect for a subset of the survivors in the study. Researchers suggested that the reason this negative effect may have occurred was because the intense memory activation aspect of the therapy may have led to a short-term increase in the awareness of all that they had experienced and endured. The researchers suggested that a longer therapeutic/storytelling process might allow the benefits of positive self-concept to reach full effect. This kind of short-term negative response, followed by a longer-term and more significant positive response, has been found by other researchers in longitudinal work (see Pennebaker, 1997).

The notation of a temporary negative self-concept effect from storytelling for survivors of IPV raises an important issue. While the potential benefits of storytelling for Elevating self-concept are indicated, such benefits are not without risk. Until the psychological processes that are involved in storytelling are more thoroughly understood in the research literature and we further understand how those processes are associated with self-concept, survivor storytelling may best be conducted in a therapeutic setting where any negative effects on self-concept can be mitigated.

Despite these potential risks, storytelling offers an invaluable opportunity for IPV survivors to reflect back on their lived experiences with violence while in the Entrapment and Escape phases and to draw conclusions, in their own words, about the various aspects of Elevation they have experienced. Current research provides evidence that narrative reflection in various forms is a valuable tool in the process of rebuilding self-concept and self-esteem.

4.3 Buttressing Self-Esteem through Service: Community Activism

Another way that IPV survivors may Elevate identity is by being of service to other survivors and by working for social change relevant to IPV. The "survivor-to-survivor model" (Wood, 2017) of service provision has deep roots in the modern social movement to end IPV. This movement has traditionally relied heavily on the services of survivors to recent victims (Pence, 2001; Wies, 2008). Researchers estimate that up to 50 percent of contemporary workers serving victims via IPV agencies are survivors themselves (Benmiller & Williams, 2011; Slattery & Goodman, 2009; Wood, 2017).

Survivor-to-survivor services have been particularly prevalent in battered women's shelters, organizations that were largely developed by this particular population (Goodman & Epstein, 2008; Schechter, 1982; Wies, 2008). A 1980 survey of 300 shelters found that almost half of the shelters employed survivors of IPV in their direct service delivery and in leadership positions on boards of directors (Roberts & Roberts, 1981). Clearly, the IPV movement has benefitted from the service and leadership of survivors, as have victims of IPV. How have the survivors themselves benefitted from their efforts, specifically in terms of their self-esteem and self-concept?

The answers to this question were explored in a qualitative study (Wood, 2017) that utilized the grounded theory method to analyze twenty-two in-depth interviews with women who worked in IPV-focused service agencies, 80 percent of whom were violence survivors. The study explored how and why the survivors were influenced by past experiences with violence in their role in serving current IPV victims. Wood determined that survivor status emerged as a major factor that influenced philosophy and approach to working with victims and how, in turn, their work with recent victims supports their own recovery and rebuilding journey. Wood described this as a "connective and circular" (p. 315) process that begins with the survivor being called to do this kind of community engagement and advocacy.

Survivors in the study identified multiple motivations for the sense of calling they felt to the survivor-to-survivor model (Wood, 2017). Personal experience with violence was one strong motivation to help others. These experiences also fostered an empathetic connection with others experiencing IPV. A second potent source of motivation was the survivors' growing awareness of the vast scope of relationship violence. The third motivation survivors expressed in the study involved social justice concerns about IPV and the lack of appropriate societal response. After describing her collective experiences with IPV, one survivor articulated the sum of these three motivations passionately (p. 317): "It permeates everything and it just always blew my mind that our society's not on fire, trying to address this."

Once the survivors began working in IPV-specific services, many of them began the process of reflecting back on their personal experiences with violence and of naming those experiences more clearly. This reflection often occurred early in their work with recent victims. One survivor described the clear lack of labeling for the violence she experienced before she began working with other IPV victims and survivors in this way (Wood, 2017, p. 317): "I didn't even know what it was called. I didn't know it had a name. I didn't know it was called 'domestic violence,' even when I was in it."

Eventually, naming the violence the survivors experienced, as well as naming the violence those they served experienced, created an opportunity to think deeply about the meaning of IPV while simultaneously establishing connections with other survivors (Wood, 2017). These connections increased empathy and supported the survivors with their self-concept and self-esteem in positive ways. One survivor commented (p. 319), "I can connect, I can relate, I can – I have empathy … I look across from me and I see me … . And I think it makes me better at this position because I don't just – I don't just know the things that I've learned in school."

Survivors who supported other victims also found other ways to use their previous experiences with IPV in positive ways (Wood, 2017). Survivorship was viewed as a model of success in living a life free from violence, as a method of building rapport with recent victims, and as a way to dismantle perceived power differentials between the recent victim and the survivor. Listening to the stories of recent victims and sharing their own stories supported the survivors' self-esteem by creating a context that increased awareness of their own progress. One survivor described how working with recent victims facilitated this awareness: "[I]t kind of makes me realize how far I've come along and just reminds me to remember where I was at one point … that I'm in a better place now" (p. 321). Wood described how the integration of the participants' former victim selves with their current survivor selves resulted in a "more holistic sense of self" (p. 322) at work, a self that served as a foundation for professionally working with recent victims. In this way, working with other victims and survivors may make one's personal Elevation progress and successes more salient.

Other researchers have noted the positive effects that serving others has on IPV survivors' self-esteem and identity. One of the subthemes that emerged in the D'Amore et al. (2018) secondary analysis of survivor writing was the idea that survivors of IPV found purpose through helping women who were experiencing that same type of violence. This Elevation of self was described in the third theme that emerged from that work, Transformation and Meaning. The research team conceptualized "meaning" as significance, referring to the survivors' construction of value and purpose in life as a result of their experiences with IPV (see also Janoff-Bulman & Yopyk, 2004). Many of the D'Amore et al. (2018) survivor narratives described how they supported other women who had experienced IPV through formal organizations or informally through friendships and how such support helped them create meaning and purpose for their experiences with violence. One survivor explained, "If I can share, one person gets helped or the next generation gets helped" (p. 14). The survivors consistently commented on the value of their IPV-related experiences, including the positive opportunity to learn about themselves, gain personal strength, reach out to others for help and support, and be a model of success for others who are currently struggling with IPV.

As we saw with storytelling, though the survivor-to-survivor model produced largely positive identity-related outcomes, there was also mention of potentially negative outcomes in this type of work. Wood (2017) notes that the survivors discussed how the close connection with recent victims could sometimes lead to boundary-setting issues. Working with recent victims also created the potential to trigger feelings tied to negative intrusive thoughts and memories for the survivor. Finally, professional burnout and "hardening" were areas of IPV survivor concern. These are commonly expressed concerns for those who work in victim-service-related fields, both for staff and volunteers who have a personal history of IPV and those who do not. Research has shown that professionals who serve IPV victims and survivors are at high risk for professional burnout, secondary traumatic stress, and compassion fatigue (Baird & Jenkins, 2003; Slattery & Goodman, 2009; Wies, 2008), possible barriers to Elevation.

Despite these potential negative outcomes, the survivor interviews (Wood, 2017) and narratives (D'Amore et al., 2018) consistently indicated that survivors who chose a path of serving others typically experienced multiple positive outcomes that buttressed their self-esteem. These results point to the potential power that serving individual victims and working toward social justice for all victims has for Elevating the self-esteem of IPV survivors.

In sum, Elevation is the final phase of the E3 Model. This phase addresses how IPV survivors experience positive changes in self-concept and self-esteem in the aftermath of violent relationships and how such rebuilding supports survivors in being happier and more hopeful. How an individual IPV survivor experiences Elevation is utterly unique. PTG theory and research attempt to understand similarities in these experiences by describing five important categories of positive change that survivors experience in the aftermath of IPV and other forms of trauma: (1) improvements in relating to others, (2) awareness of new possibilities, (3) an increased sense of personal strength, (4) positive spiritual and existential change, and (5) a renewed appreciation of life. Other aspects of Elevation may be experienced and promoted through the process of writing and sharing one's story. Storytelling reveals other important aspects of Elevation IPV survivors may experience, including (1) an increased ability to discern the self, (2) positive changes in self-concept and self-esteem, and (3) significantly increased levels of positive affect, including feelings of happiness, contentment, and hope for the future for themselves and their children. Another important path to Elevation for IPV survivors is to be of service to other victims and through the process of working for justice and social change on IPV-related issues. Such efforts have a tremendously positive effect on survivors' self-concept and self-esteem. Additional paths may be discovered by future research.

Regardless of which aspects of Elevation are described, or which paths survivors followed to achieve these positive effects, the Elevation phase of the E3 Model indicates that a positive legacy can result from negative experiences as survivors bravely seek to make sense of the senseless acts of violence they experienced in their relationships.

5 Applications and Future Research

This Element will close by discussing forms of social support that may help IPV survivors evolve through the phases of Entrapment, Escape, and Enlightenment. We also suggest systemic and policy changes that may support survivors and their children. Finally, we discuss the limitations of the current research and promising future directions. These recommendations are summarized briefly in Table 1 and are further expanded upon in the sections that follow. How can social psychological research inform practice so that survivors are more likely to move through the three phases suggested in the E3 Model? In a world in which 47 percent of men and women experience psychological or physical abuse from a partner in their lifetime (National Center for Victims of Crime, 2018), it is important to understand how survivors grow and develop more positive identities in the aftermath of IPV and how both scholars and society can better help.

5.1 Social Support

A survivor's response to the experience of IPV is multidimensional and deeply personal due to the serious effects the violence has on them physically, mentally, emotionally, and spiritually (D'Amore et al., 2018). Given this complexity, survivors' needs for support are highly individualized and may change as they move through the process of Entrapment, Escape, and Elevation. It is important to recognize the role of social support as a way to facilitate the growth and positive identity that is possible while a survivor is still involved in an abusive relationship (Cobb et al., 2006; D'Amore et al, 2018), after the survivor leaves such relationships (Cobb et al., 2006; Ulloa et al., 2015), and while the survivor is in the process of creating meaning and experiencing growth from the trauma of IPV (Bakaityte et al., 2020; Jenks, 2014).

Social support is defined as assistance, both emotional and practical, from other individuals in a wide variety of forms (Taylor, 2011). It is a beneficial factor in IPV survivors' decisions to leave a violent relationship and in positive adjustment following their exposure to trauma (Coker et al., 2004; Estrellado & Loh, 2014; Song, 2012; Zapor et al., 2015). The social support of family and friends provides important resources during the process of identity exploration, especially during the early years of an individual's life (Dumas et al., 2009). These same social relationships may be critical for IPV survivors later in life because of the shattering effect violent relationships have on survivors' identities (Bakaityte et al., 2020). Supportive friends and family may best serve by helping IPV survivors leave their previous "self" behind and, instead, build a "whole new understanding about themselves" (Bakaityte et al., 2020, p. 4).

It is important, however, to distinguish between helpful social support and unhelpful social support. This is especially true for IPV victims who are snared in the Entrapment phase of a violent relationship. Research on female victims of IPV suggests that disclosure of violence to family members can sometimes lead to further victimization and may negatively influence a victim's decision to stay in or leave a violent relationship (Estrellado & Loh, 2014). Indeed, Rosen's (1996) original discussion of Entrapment included an analysis of "family collusion," in which family members actually encourage victims to stay in the relationship for various reasons (such as religion or financial benefits). Such unhealthy attempts at support may increase safety risks for an IPV victim and

Table 1 Application of the E3 Model for practitioners, policy makers, and researchers

E3 Phase	Social Support	Systemic Support	Future Research
Entrapment	Educational outreach that teaches family and friends about the dynamics of IPV and the importance of not blaming victims	Widespread societal education that challenges IPV-related myths and accurately portrays the experience of victims and their children and warning signs of future abuse	Interdisciplinary quantitative research that focuses on the lived experience of diverse populations of IPV victims and children and relevant cultural messages
Escape	Educational outreach that teaches family and friends how to support victims in safely leaving violent relationships when they are ready	Creating access to IPV-specific advocates to assist survivors and their children in negotiating complex legal and social systems and services	Quantitative research regarding the gaps in survivor services and how those gaps affect victims and their children during the escape
Elevation	Educational outreach that teaches family and friends how to acknowledge survivor strengths and support survivors in galvanizing self-esteem	Programs that foster survivor-to-survivor connection and create opportunities to safely voice requests for change and expression of newfound strengths	Quantitative research regarding how survivor-to-survivor service and storytelling correlate with positive self-concept and self-esteem in the wake of IPV

Note: The three phases of the E3 Model may not always be distinct from one another (stages can overlap) and an individual's progression through the phases may not be linear (progression can go back and forth). Each IPV survivor's experience of the Entrapment, Escape, and Elevation phases is unique.

diminish their potential for becoming a survivor by Escaping the relationship or of experiencing Elevated growth and positive identity changes.

The potential negative effect of unhelpful social support may extend to IPV victims who enter the Escape phase as well. Because IPV relationships tend to be cyclical in nature (Walker, 1984), victims who seek to Escape may go through periods of time when they struggle with whether to stay or leave a relationship (Copp et al., 2015). This process of decision-making can create challenges for family and friends who may be less likely to offer helpful support to victims when such dynamics develop (Goodkind et al., 2003). This kind of unhelpful support may therefore create barriers for people trying to move from the Escape phase to the Elevation phase.

Those caveats aside, other recent research has examined how effective social support facilitates new positive survivor identities after experiencing the traumatic events of IPV. Zukauskiene et al. (2021) examined the role of social support in the development of both PTG and identity reconsideration for 217 victims of IPV. The research team found that helpful social support, but not unhelpful social support, positively correlated with all identity processes assessed in the study. Specifically, these processes supported positive self-image via ruminative exploration (e.g., "I keep wondering which direction my life has to take"), identification with commitment (e.g., "Because of my future plans I feel certain about myself"), commitment making (e.g., "I have decided on the direction I am going to follow in my life"), exploration in breadth (e.g., "I am considering a number of different lifestyles that might suit me"), and exploration in depth (e.g., "I think about the future plans I already made"). The study concluded that healthy, helpful social support fostered evaluation of the survivors' current identities and the formation of new identities. It also found that unhelpful support may not play any role in the reconsideration of a survivor's identity and does not mitigate the positive effects of helpful social support.

The need for social support, in general, was recently articulated in a study examining the "learned experience" of long-term IPV survivors (Flasch et al., 2020, p. 29). This study sought to understand the messages long-term survivors of IPV wanted to send others who have recently left an abusive relationship. Survivors responded to open-ended questions, their statements coalescing into eleven primary themes. Of those eleven themes, the need for social support was the third most important one described. Particularly desired was informal support from friends, family, and mentors. Subthemes that emerged under the general topic of social support emphasized the fact that social support is indeed available and that survivors must allow themselves to accept such support. One participant encouraged, "Surround yourself with people that support you and believe you" (p. 35). In this way, self-image must include an acknowledgment that vulnerability and the need for social support are normal and that seeking help indicates identity strength instead of weakness.

Another subtheme that emerged was a caution to recognize unhelpful social support, recommendations to avoid such support, and encouragement to new survivors to distance themselves from individuals who are not helpful (Flasch et al., 2020). One survivor warned, "People will want to impose their views of your journey and when you are vulnerable . . . be aware" (p. 35). This caution is supported by other studies (e.g., Estrellado & Loh, 2014; Rosen, 1996) documenting the effect that unhelpful family members had on victims, specifically how such negative forms of support may actually encourage a victim to stay trapped in a violent relationship. These studies emphasize that survivor self-image must be formed by the individuals themselves to be empowering, not formed from judgments or labels delivered by others.

One final message from the survivors in the Flasch et al. (2020) study is consistent with the research cited previously regarding the value of survivor-to-survivor support as a path to Elevation (D'Amore et al., 2018; Wood, 2017). The subtheme "seek out other survivors" encouraged social support from others who have had similar experiences. One survivor encouraged this form of connectivity by stating, "Seek others who have been through it too and learn from them. Support each other" (p. 35). Shared experiences with the identity evolution in the E3 Model can help people move through and maintain their forward progress.

Taken in sum, the above research indicates that social support for IPV survivors has the potential to be helpful, unhelpful, or nonexistent. Because helpful social support is linked to both growth and positive identity reformation (Zukauskiene et al., 2021), the importance of support from a variety of social contacts and networks for IPV survivors cannot be underestimated. In addition to support needing to actually be helpful in terms of being empathetic and empowering, particular types of support may be needed by different survivors at different phases. Four specific types of social support have been identified in psychological literature (House, 1981), including (1) emotional support, such as hugging someone when they cry; (2) instrumental support, such as providing a place for people to live or providing transportation; (3) informational support, such as helping people navigate the criminal justice and courts systems; and (4) appraisal support, which is tied to helping people grow and praising them for moving toward personal goals. All four types may be critical to Elevation.

Increased understanding of the type of social support that aids the recovery of IPV survivors is important for family, friends, practitioners, service providers, and policy makers. Researchers can assist in this process by further exploring how different types of social support – from whom – are linked to self-concept, self-esteem, and identity reformation for current victims in the Entrapment phase, burgeoning survivors as they determine how and when to Escape, and survivors who have left violent relationships behind and are seeking positive growth and Elevation. Further explorations of what survivors need to evolve through these phases and the types of research that may be most helpful to support this evolution are discussed in the sections below.

5.2 Systemic Support

What do IPV survivors have to teach us, especially about the systems that are in place to support them, or the lack thereof? Listening to the lived experiences of survivors is one of the surest ways that family, friends, researchers, helping professionals, communities, and policy makers can improve systemic support to IPV survivors during all three of the E3 phases and ultimately prevent such violence from happening to others (see Table 1).

Cerulli et al. (2015) designed a qualitative study that sought to understand the need for systemic change in services to victims by interviewing IPV survivors. The study method involved seven in-depth focus groups: four in the Midwest and three in upstate New York. Researchers invited survivors to share their experiences with community-coordinated systems and further to provide insight into how systemic support could be improved. Findings from the focus groups encompassed four domains of needed change: (1) individual, (2) relationship, (3) community, and (4) societal. Researchers emphasized that "improved education on understanding and addressing IPV surfaced across all domains" (p. 80).

Survivors were clear that some of the needed systemic changes were individual (Cerulli et al., 2015). They described needing to be more educated about what resources were locally available. They also, however, noted that many existing community systems are perceived as complex and intimidating. Thus, they noted that it was imperative that survivors had professional guidance in negotiating these systems so they were better able to help themselves. Specifically, they suggested having IPV-specific court advocates available, support groups to connect them to other survivors, and safe places to access mental health services.

The relationship domain emphasized the importance of helpful social support, both professional and nonprofessional (Cerulli et al., 2015). Key relationships identified were IPV-specific advocates, family members (including family members of the abusive former partners), and children. Survivors in the focus groups were highly concerned about their children. They expressed a strong desire to have their children learn about the dynamics of IPV and learn how to build healthy relationships to reduce the intergenerational transmission of violence.

Survivors discussed the need for community-level change as well (Cerulli et al., 2015). In general, they expressed strong support for IPV-specific courts, interdisciplinary coalitions, and legislation that better recognizes the needs of IPV victims and survivors. The focus groups articulated strong support for coordinated community responses to IPV and for specialized, high-level training programs for service providers who are involved in interdisciplinary efforts. Survivors also discussed specific logistical needs when accessing specialized courts. Examples were having separate parking lots with escorts for safety purposes, separate access doors for survivors and perpetrators, staggered arrival times, and separate security clearance systems in the courts so survivors didn't have to interact with perpetrators during judicial proceedings.

The societal-level changes that survivors discussed focused on altering the way IPV is portrayed to more accurately describe their experiences (Cerulli et al., 2015). One specific suggestion included renaming IPV to "domestic terrorism." Another suggestion involved creating a surveillance system for IPV offenders, similar to those utilized to catch sex abusers and other predators through public media outlets. Survivors emphasized that society in general needs to be more aware of IPV and more educated about the dynamics of such violence. They believed that public recognition and involvement would help prevent IPV at the societal level.

These thoughtful insights and suggestions may be drawn upon to inform research, outreach and education efforts, service delivery, and policy development. We also suggest consideration of the following specific systemic changes within the context of Entrapment, Escape, and Elevation. As noted previously, the word "entrapment" was first utilized by Rosen (1996) to describe how IPV victims are initially attracted to abusers and then kept in abusive relationships. Survivors' self-concept in this phase of evolution is heavily influenced by culture and the romantic myths that may contribute to the Entrapment of victims (e.g., Cava et al., 2020; Masanet et al., 2018; Sánchez-Hernández et al., 2020). The antidote to these cultural influences, and the corresponding negative impact on self-concept, may lie in early and widespread societal education about the warning signs of potentially violent relationships.

Such preventative education, delivered in a developmentally appropriate manner to young children through college-aged young adults, may serve to counter culturally promoted myths that underlie victim Entrapment. In addition, teaching practical cognitive models of violent versus healthy relationship dynamics may support survivors in overcoming the cognitive reframing process that often corresponds with IPV and maintains victim Entrapment. Such models may also promote accurate and healthy self-perception that supports individuals when/if they encounter abusive behavior.

The additional curriculum could be developed targeting older students in secondary and postsecondary settings that teaches about the dynamics of IPV and the difference between helpful versus unhelpful social support. This kind of programming could be parallel to the "bystander intervention" training currently popular on college and university campuses regarding sexual assault (e.g., Coker et al., 2011; Henriksen et al., 2015; Senn & Forrest, 2016). Education programs could explain how a victim may be manipulated by an abusive partner over time to the point that the victim's motivation and sense of self have been reduced to helplessness. Teaching others what to say and do to help victims help themselves, combined with education about local and national resources, creates a promising avenue for supporting victims in moving beyond Entrapment.

Widespread education programs, delivered through public education, offer multiple potential benefits. First, preventative education that teaches people how to recognize and respond to the early warning signs of a potentially violent relationship may function as a protective mechanism to help reduce the intergenerational transmission of IPV. Second, public education programs regarding the dynamics of relationship violence and the development of healthy, nonviolent relationships may address victim anxiety about the welfare of their children, thus enhancing the possibility of increased victim attention to self. Finally, such programs, over time, would enhance the percentage of social supporters in our society who are capable of interacting with IPV victims in a genuinely helpful manner. Helpful social support is invaluable for assisting victims in repairing fractured identities and for encouraging victims to move toward Escape and through Elevation, as described previously.

The previously cited Cerulli et al. (2015) study directed strong attention to the value of IPV-supportive public policy and intervention. While social support is invaluable in each phase of survivor evolution, especially as such support relates to issues of rebuilding self-concept and self-esteem, public policies and programs may be the most important supportive factors when it comes time for a victim of IPV to become a survivor and finally Escape a violent relationship.

Survivor concerns about children and the relationships they have with those children in the aftermath of IPV are well documented in the literature (e.g., Cerulli et al., 2015; D'Amore et al., 2018). Anxiety over children may come to the forefront as victims make the transition to becoming survivors and worry about whether their children will transition with them. One of the most important reasons victims stay in violent relationships is fear of losing custody of their children (Kurz, 1995). This fear is well founded according to the Leadership Council on Child Abuse and Interpersonal Violence (2008), which estimates that every year in the United States, 58,000 children are placed in the custody, often unsupervised, of an abuser by family courts. The end result is that IPV survivors finally get away from their abusive partners and then are forced by the courts to leave their children behind, open and vulnerable to the same abuse from which they Escaped.

A recent study conducted an in-depth analysis of twenty-seven "turned around" custody cases in which US family courts initially placed children in the custody of an abusive parent and later reversed those decisions, returning the children to the survivor parent (Silberg & Dallam, 2019). The average time a child was subjected to the court-ordered custody of an abusive parent was 3.2 years. The study found that during this time, 88% of the children reported incidents of abuse. Furthermore, the children's mental and physical health deteriorated to the point that 33% of the children became suicidal, 33% experienced depression, and 13% engaged in self-harm. When survivors sought to protect their children by raising abuse concerns to the family courts, their efforts were regarded with suspicion. In addition, two-thirds of the parents who raised issues of concern were pathologized by the court for advocating for child safety. This finding is consistent with other studies regarding how family courts tend to respond negatively to IPV survivors who raise abuse concerns about their children and render less than favorable custody rulings to survivor parents (Kernic et al., 2005; Saccuzzo & Johnson, 2004).

Silberg and Dallam (2019) made numerous policy recommendations as a result of their analysis, including the suggestions that family courts be required to resolve safety risks and claims of violence first (before determining child custody), that friendly parent custodial provisions be rendered inapplicable to custody cases that allege IPV and/or child abuse, and finally that children who disclose abuse be court-referred for evaluation from professionals who have specialized training in IPV and other forms of family violence. While an examination of all IPV-related policies is beyond the scope of this Element, the custody-related issue discussed here is one example of the policy and systemic changes that need to be implemented in order for IPV survivors to truly Escape from abuse and to be better supported in seeking violence-free lives and Elevated selves.

We wish to note, however, that regardless of the social or systemic support available to them, every year thousands of IPV survivors find a way to somehow overcome the practical and emotional reasons why they should not leave an abuser including deficits in financial resources; cultural pressures; barriers created by friends, family, and other social networks; lack of legal resources; overwhelming fears about the physical and psychological safety of their children in the custody of abusers; lack of employment training; pressing medical needs; depletion of the psychological resources that are needed to make decisions; deficits in physical protection from the abusive partners they are leaving; lack of housing; and significant IPV-related mental health challenges (Arias & Pape, 1999; Fugate et al., 2005; Kirkwood, 1993; Mookerjee et al., 2015; Overstreet & Quinn, 2013; Rodriguez et al., 2010; Rolling & Brosi, 2010). Despite these challenges, they reclaim their lost selves, rebuild their fractured identities, and grow into happier, healthier, more hopeful individuals.

Perhaps what IPV survivors' lived experience has to teach us most thoroughly is perseverance in the face of overwhelming adversity. And perhaps what we, as researchers, friends, and family members, owe them most is admiration and our best effort to facilitate social and systemic changes that help survivors help themselves and their children.

5.3 Future Research

Much of the work already done with IPV survivors is qualitative in nature with small sample sizes (e.g., Brosi et al., 2020; D'Amore et al., 2018; Rosen, 1996; Wood, 2017). A number of recent qualitative studies have expanded the number of participants; for example, Flasch et al. (2020) analyzed results from 263 survivors, and Bakaityte et al. (2020) surveyed 221 survivors. Larger, more representative samples support more robust findings and should be encouraged. The field would also benefit from more use of quantitative research methods, especially experimental manipulation; an example in this Element is the study by Moreira et al. (2020) that utilized a randomized controlled trial design. However, because of the inherent vulnerability of this research population, experimental methods must be carefully designed and implemented. Quantitative research may benefit from interdisciplinary teams that represent different perspectives on survivor vulnerabilities. Despite the challenges, quantitative design is an important method of research to pursue to increase our understanding of the experience and needs of this diverse population.

While helping victims and survivors of IPV is essential, the ideal solution would be to prevent it from happening in the first place. To achieve this goal, more research is also needed on the psychology of perpetrators. Many scholars have contributed to this goal by suggesting frameworks for why violence erupts within relationships, such as the helpful I^3 Model (e.g., Finkel, 2008, 2014; Johnson, 1995, 2007), personality or attitude factors in perpetrators that are associated with aggression (e.g., Herzberger & Rueckert, 1997; Jacobson & Gottman, 1998), mental health problems in perpetrators (e.g., Dutton, 1998; Holtzworth-Munroe & Meehan, 2004; Holtzworth-Munroe & Stuart, 1994; Holtzworth-Munroe et al., 2000), and intergenerational transmission of IPV within families (Dunlap et al., 2002; Stith et al., 2000). In terms of self-esteem, results have been conflicting regarding whether perpetrators abuse their partners due to haunting low self-esteem, narcissist high self-esteem, or unstable and therefore volatile self-esteem (see Baumeister et al., 2000). A promising line of work regarding perpetrator identity within culture also points to toxic masculinity within a "culture of honor" in which violent values are incorporated into one's sense of self (e.g., Baldry et al., 2013; Dietrich & Schuett, 2013; Lowe et al., 2018; Marín-Morales et al., 2020; Senkans et al., 2020). All of these ideas need further exploration to determine the best ways to understand and treat perpetrators and – ideally – intervene before the aggression begins.

We now shift focus to future research within the three phases of survivor evolution proposed in the E3 Model (see the final column of Table 1). People in the Entrapment phase, perhaps more than those in any of the other phases proposed, may be most vulnerable to social messaging, whether it be through romantic myths and fantasies (Cava et al., 2020; Jackson, 2001; Rosen, 1996) or unhelpful messages directly from family (Estrellado & Loh, 2014). The experience of being trapped in a violent relationship, with constant accompanying psychological abuse, leads to an erosion of the self (Matheson et al., 2015). More research is needed regarding how different forms of social support, helpful and unhelpful, influence self-concept and self-esteem for survivors in this vulnerable stage. Zukauskiene et al. (2021) highlighted the importance of social support after experiencing IPV to support the development of new positive identities in survivors. Additional research should explore how social support effects are mediated and moderated by other relevant variables, such as individual or cultural differences, and how these forms of support are tied to self-image and identity. Comprehensive research that explores social support for victims who also suffer from systemic disadvantages and discrimination would greatly increase understanding of how social support bolsters and diminishes victim identity in the Entrapment phase. Such research would inform practice so that a more diverse range of victims could be supported in moving to the next phase – Escape.

As noted in the previous section, IPV survivors who are in the Escape phase are likely to benefit from policies and coordinated systems that facilitate ending their abusive relationships safely while simultaneously beginning the process of rebuilding a new self that has the potential for growth. The importance of systems and policies in this transition period was emphasized by Cerulli et al. (2015) in survivor interviews that discussed needed systemic changes at the individual, relationship, community, and societal levels. Building on what survivor-lived experience has taught us about gaps in these areas, future research should explore how IPV-related education programs that are created for survivors influence identity during periods of Escape.

This Element explored the research that describes three mechanisms of support that facilitate survivor Elevation: PTG, narrative storytelling, and survivor-to-survivor service. The phenomenon of PTG in IPV survivors has been documented in qualitative literature (Anderson et al., 2012; Senter & Caldwell, 2002). Additional literature has outlined how positive identity development may possibly influence the process of PTG (Joireman et al., 2002, Zukauskiene et al., 2021). Future research should explore how identity development and redevelopment emerge in the wake of IPV and the correlational versus causal association between IPV and PTG.

Trauma survivors may experience benefits including improved self-concept through storytelling (Orang et al., 2018; Pennebaker, 1997; Sharma-Patel et al., 2012; Volpe et al., 2017). What is unclear at this time is how and why narrative therapy benefits IPV survivors from an identity development point of view. Though limited research has recently begun the process of exploring these questions (e.g., Moreira et al., 2020), this is an area of investigation that warrants further attention.

Survivors appear to thrive when they serve the needs of other survivors (D'Amore et al., 2018; Jordan, 2003; Kirkwood, 1993; Wood, 2017). However, there is also literature that suggests that survivors may experience negative outcomes from the same type of service (Slattery & Goodman, 2009). Additional research is needed to clarify how self-concept and self-esteem are influenced by survivor-to-survivor service and what moderators are most likely to help this kind of service be beneficial to all involved. More work is also needed on how other aspects of Elevation might not be covered by the aspects discussed in PTG, storytelling, and helping others.

In addition to research on the specific phases of survivor evolution suggested in this Element, longitudinal research is needed regarding identity-related issues as individuals progress from the Entrapment phase of being a victim, through the Escape phase that leads to becoming a survivor, and finally to the reintegration of new identity and psychological growth that characterize Elevation. Parallel research could be done to see how social support and other forms of systemic support accompany changes in self-concept and self-esteem. Such research would explore IPV survivor identity as the recovery process continues in one's life.

Most importantly, the E3 Model explicitly notes that movement through and between phases can go in either direction, that phases can overlap, and that different people will go through the phases on different timelines depending on their individual situations. Most of the research we reviewed in this Element discusses a single point in time within the overall model, but future research needs to clarify how people successfully move through. Work might be done on individual differences in timelines and trajectories along the phases of the E3 Model, helping explain why some people may progress slower or faster or whether progress occurs in slow and small steps versus larger but more intermittent steps.

It is essential to note that not everyone does successfully Escape from IPV and that some people who do never psychologically recover their best selves or self-esteem. How to help people transition through to the final stages is therefore key.

6 Conclusions

This Element presents a novel framework called the E3 Model. It organizes current research on the experience of IPV and how people can evolve from IPV victims (Entrapment) to survivors (Escape) to individuals with a fully healed and empowered self (Elevation). The E3 Model emphasizes the transcendence of IPV and personal growth. Social psychology has long been studying identity and intimate relationship dynamics but most often as two separate areas of research. The IPV phenomenon presents a uniquely fascinating and alarming juxtaposition of the two subjects. As shown in Figure 1, the phases outlined in the E3 Model are depicted as overlapping. People may be psychologically shifting between phases and may temporarily move backward – but the overall progression is forward for people who eventually reach Elevation.

While psychological research in and of itself cannot create social or systemic changes, it is invaluable for informing practice in such a way that changes are guided by survivors' lived experiences and by evidence. This is one important way that research supports IPV survivors. This Element has reviewed the current body of research in the context of three phases of survivor experience – Entrapment, Escape, and Elevation – specifically in terms of identity, self-concept, and self-esteem. Though social psychology is the lens through which this body of work was reviewed, it is important to note that many applicable studies are conducted in other academic fields including social work, criminal justice, public health, clinical psychology, gender studies, communication, experimental psychology, human services, family studies, and medicine.

Future research will benefit from a continued interdisciplinary approach to understanding the experience and needs of IPV survivors.

Such research will also benefit from continuously expanding the definition of "survivor" to be more inclusive. The vast majority of research on IPV survivors has focused on female survivors. While this focus is understandable given the general ratio of female IPV survivors to other genders, a continuing effort must be made to include all survivors in the research process. When one in ten men in the United States has been the target of sexual and/or physical violence from a partner, it is a population that cannot be ignored or discounted (NCADV, 2020). A similar effort is needed to expand IPV research beyond heterosexual and cisgender survivors so that we understand the dynamics of IPV in gender-diverse and sexually diverse populations and are able to identify specific needs these communities may have. Some research indicates that rates of IPV may be even higher in LGBTQ+ relationships, compared to heterosexual relationships; this population needs just as much support, if not more (see Baker et al., 2013; Kimmes et al., 2019; Messinger, 2011; West, 1998).

Survivors have emphasized how complicated and confusing IPV-related systems and policies are and have stressed the need for guiding resources that can help survivors negotiate these systems (Cerulli et al., 2015). They have also emphasized the fact that many of them are unable to leave their abusive homes in order to obtain education and resources. These survivor-identified needs could be addressed by designing research that utilizes online or phone app technologies to link survivors to education and resources while simultaneously evaluating how such education affects self-concept and self-identity. Support and analysis could begin during the Escape phase and follow survivors longitudinally as they progress through Elevation.

We made a concerted effort in this Element to include studies that focused on survivors from different cultures (Bakaityte et al., 2020; Moreira et al., 2020; Orang et al., 2018; Zukauskiene et al., 2021) in order to create a more culturally diverse analysis. This practice should be encouraged to increase our understanding of individuals who also suffer from systemic disadvantages (i.e., due to their membership in a traditionally oppressed group such as immigrants, people of color, individuals with disabilities, and so on). IPV-related research regarding how socioeconomic class impacts survivors in all three phases of evolution – Entrapment, Escape, and Elevation – is significantly lacking. This is an area of research that needs to be developed.

Social psychological theory can also be used for future work. Theories briefly outlined earlier suggest that self-image and identity change once a committed relationship is formed (e.g., self-expansion theory; Aron & Aron, 1986; interdependence theory; Kelley & Thibaut, 1978; cognitive interdependence theory;

Agnew et al., 1998). These theoretical backdrops could each be used in interesting ways to explore specific parts of movement through the phases of the E3 Model. For example, studies based on cognitive interdependence theory find that as commitment in a relationship grows, we move from using singular pronouns like "I" and "my" to inclusive pronouns like "we" and "our" (e.g., Goodfriend & Agnew, 2008). At what point in Entrapment, Escape, and Elevation do these identity-relevant pronouns shift? Another example is that interdependence theory suggests people are more likely to leave relationships if they perceive viable alternatives, but alternatives can be missed if an abusive partner has eroded self-esteem enough (Arriaga et al., 2013). Again, it would be worthwhile to explore how and when perceived alternatives shift as survivors realize their partners may be purposely manipulating their views. Does an increased perception of positive alternatives help one Escape, or does this happen more in the Elevation phase through PTG?

All of these suggestions may help prevent and respond to IPV in ways that truly matter to individuals. Being the target of abuse from the one you love is devastating to someone's identity, self-concept, and self-esteem. While an interdisciplinary approach will be necessary to ameliorate IPV, social psychology is a key discipline in which scholars are particularly suited to offer theory and empirical evidence regarding the phenomenon. Ending IPV is not just an academic endeavor; it is one that touches millions of individual lives every day.

One goal we have in creating the E3 Model is that it may be useful for practitioners working with targets of IPV, to show the personal evolution that is possible. While the I³ Model offers predictors of when IPV is more or less likely to occur (Finkel, 2008, 2014; Finkel & Hall, 2018; Finkel et al., 2012), the E3 Model focuses specifically on the evolution and transcendence of experiencing IPV and how that abuse affects identity, self-concept, and self-esteem. Sharing research on overcoming the Entrapment and Escape phases with current victims and survivors may inspire and help them make the transition to Elevation. We also hope the E3 Model offers some small insight into the scope of the problem, extant issues in social structure and policy, and future research which may scaffold optimism that IPV can be decreased, if not eliminated. While extraordinary research advances have occurred in the last century or so, much more is needed.

References

Agnew, C. R., Van Lange, P. A., Rusbult, C. E., & Langston, C. A. (1998). Cognitive interdependence: Commitment and the mental representation of close relationships. *Journal of Personality and Social Psychology, 74*(4), 939–954. https://doi.org/10.1037/0022-3514.74.4.939

Akangbe Tomisin, A. (2020). Culture, religion and help-seeking for intimate partner violence victims in Nigeria: A narrative review. *Culture, 3*(2), 56–62.

Allen-Collinson, J. (2009). A marked man: A case of female-perpetrated intimate partner abuse. *International Journal of Men's Health, 8*(1), 22–40. https://doi.org/10.1177/1077801212470543

Anderson, K. M., Renner, L. M., & Danis, F. S. (2012). Recovery: Resilience and growth in the aftermath of domestic violence. *Violence against Women, 18*(11), 1279–1299. https://doi.org/10.1177/1077801212470543

Arias, I., & Pape, K. T. (1999). Psychological abuse: Implications for adjustment and commitment to leave violent partners. *Violence and Victims, 14*(1), 55–67. https://doi.org/10.1891/08866708.14.1.55

Arnocky, S., & Vaillancourt, T. (2014). Sex differences in response to victimization by an intimate partner: More stigmatization and less help-seeking among males. *Journal of Aggression, Maltreatment & Trauma, 23*(7), 705–724. https://doi.org/10.1080/10926771.2014.933465

Aron, A., & Aron, E. N. (1986). *Love and the expansion of self: Understanding attraction and satisfaction*. Hemisphere.

Arriaga, X. B. (2002). Joking violence among highly committed individuals. *Journal of Interpersonal Violence, 17*(6), 591–610. https://doi.org/10.1177/0886260502017006001

Arriaga, X. B., Capezza, N. M., Goodfriend, W., Rayl, E. S., & Sands, K. J. (2013). Individual well-being and relationship maintenance at odds: The unexpected perils of maintaining a relationship with an aggressive partner. *Social Psychological and Personality Science, 4*(6), 676–684. https://doi.org/10.1177/1948550613480822

Baird, S., & Jenkins, S. R. (2003). Vicarious traumatization, secondary traumatic stress, and assault and domestic violence agency staff. *Violence and Victims, 18*(1), 71–86. https://doi.org/10.1891/vivi.2003.18.1.71

Bakaityte, A., Kaniusonyte, G., Truskauskaite-Kuneviciene, I., & Zukauskiene, R. (2020). Longitudinal investigation of posttraumatic growth in female survivors of intimate partner violence: The role of event centrality and identity exploration. *Journal of Interpersonal Violence*, [online], 1–19. https://doi.org/10.1177/0886260520920864

Baker, N. L., Buick, J. D., Kim, S. R., Moniz, S., & Nava, K. L. (2013). Lessons from examining same-sex intimate partner violence. *Sex Roles*, *69*(3–4), 182–192. https://doi.org/10.1007/s11199-0120218-3

Baldry, A. C., Pagliaro, S., & Porcaro, C. (2013). The rule of law at time of masculine honor: Afghan police attitudes and intimate partner violence. *Group Processes & Intergroup Relations*, *16*(3), 363–374. https://doi.org/10.1177/1368430212462492

Bandura, A. (1986). *Social foundations of thought and action: A social cognitive theory.* Prentice-Hall.

Basile, K. C., Arias, I., Desai, S., & Thompson, M. P. (2004). The differential association of intimate partner physical, sexual, psychological, and stalking violence and posttraumatic stress symptoms in a nationally representative sample of women. *Journal of Traumatic Stress*, *17*(5), 413–421. https://doi.org/10.1023/B:JOTS.0000048954.50232.d8

Baumeister, R. F., Bushman, B. J., & Campbell, W. K. (2000). Self-esteem, narcissism, and aggression: Does violence result from low self-esteem or from threatened egotism? *Current Directions in Psychological Science*, *9*(1), 26–29. https://doi.org/10.1111/1467-8721.00053

Baumeister, R. F., Smart, L., & Boden, J. M. (1996). Relation of threatened egotism to violence and aggression: The dark side of high self-esteem. *Psychological Review*, *103*(1), 5–33. https://doi.org/10.1037/0033-295X.103.1.5

Bem, D. J. (1967). Self-perception: An alternative interpretation of cognitive dissonance phenomena. *Psychological Review*, *74*(3), 183–200. https://doi.org/10.1037/h0024835

Benmiller, M., & Williams, L. S. (2011). The role of adaptation in advocate burnout: A case for good soldiering. *Violence against Women*, *17*(1), 89–110. https://doi.org/10.1177/1077801210393923

Beydoun, H. A., Beydoun, M. A., Kaufman, J. S., Lo, B., & Zonderman, A. B. (2012). Intimate partner violence against adult women and its association with major depressive disorder, depressive symptoms and postpartum depression: A systematic review and meta-analysis. *Social Science & Medicine*, *75*(6), 959–975. https://doi.org/10.1016/j.socscimed.2012.04.025

Braun, V., & Clarke, V. (2006). Using thematic analysis in psychology. *Qualitative Research in Psychology*, *3*(2), 77–101. https://doi.org/10.1191/1478088706qp063oa

Brewer, M. B. (2001). The many faces of social identity: Implications for political psychology. *Political Psychology*, *22*(1), 115–125. https://doi.org/10.1111/0162-895X.00229

Brosi, M., Rolling, E., Gaffney, C., & Kitch, B. (2020). Beyond resilience: Glimpses into women's posttraumatic growth after experiencing intimate partner violence. *The American Journal of Family Therapy, 48*(1), 1–15. https://doi.org/10.1080/019226187.2019.1691084

Brownridge, D. A., Taillieu, T., Urquia, M. L. et al. (2020). Intimate partner violence among persons with mental health-related disabilities in Canada. *Journal of Interpersonal Violence*, [online], 1–23. https://doi.org/10.1177/0886260520912589

Buehler, R., & McFarland, C. (2001). Intensity bias in affective forecasting: The role of temporal focus. *Personality and Social Psychology Bulletin, 27*(11), 1480–1493. https://doi.org/10.1177/01461672012711009

Calhoun, L. G., & Tedeschi, R. G. (1998). Posttraumatic growth: Future directions. In R. G. Tedeschi, C. L. Park, & L. G. Calhoun (Eds.), *Posttraumatic growth: Positive change in the aftermath of crisis* (pp. 215–238). Lawrence Erlbaum.

Campbell, R., Dworkin, E., & Cabral, G. (2009). An ecological model of the impact of sexual assault on women's mental health. *Trauma, Violence, & Abuse, 10*(3), 225–246. https://doi.org/10.1177/1524838009334456

Cava, M. J., Buelga, S., Carrascosa, L., & Ortega-Barón, J. (2020). Relations among romantic myths, offline dating violence victimization and cyber dating violence victimization in adolescents. *International Journal of Environmental Research and Public Health, 17*(5), Article e1551. https://doi.org/10.3390/ijerph17051551

Cerulli, C., Trabold, N., Kothari, C. L. et al. (2015). In our voice: Survivors' recommendations for change. *Journal of Family Violence, 30*, 75–83. https://doi.org/10.1007/s10896-014-9657-7

Choi, A. W. (2020). Validation of the scale for assessing the psychological vulnerability and its association with health of intimate partner violence victims in Chinese young adult population. *PLoS One, 15*(7), Article e0235761. https://doi.org/10.1371/journal.pone.0235761

Clulow, C. (2012). *Adult attachment and couple psychotherapy: The "secure base" in practice and research*. Brunner-Routledge.

Cobb, A. R., Tedeschi, R. G., Calhoun, L. G., & Cann, A. (2006). Correlates of post-traumatic growth in survivors of intimate partner violence. *Journal of Traumatic Stress, 19*(6), 895–903. https://doi.org/10.1002/jts.20171

Coker, A. L., Cook-Craig, P. G., Williams, C. M. et al. (2011). Evaluation of Green Dot: An active bystander intervention to reduce sexual violence on college campuses. *Violence against Women, 17*(6), 777–796. https://doi.org/10.1177/1077801211410264

Coker, A. L., Smith, P. H., Thompson, M. P. et al. (2004). Social support protects against the negative effects of partner violence on mental health. *Journal of Women's Health & Gender-Based Medicine, 11*(5), 465–476. https://doi.org/10.1089/15246090260137644

Cooper, A., & Smith, E. L. (2011). *Homicide trends in the United States, 1980–2008*. US Department of Justice. https://bjs.ojp.gov/content/pub/pdf/htus8008.pdf

Copp, J. E., Giordano, P. C., Longmore, M. A., & Manning, W. D. (2015). Stay-or-leave decision making in nonviolent and violent dating relationships. *Violence and Victims*, *30*(4), 581–599. https://doi.org/10.1891/0886-6708.VV-D-13-00176

Costa, E. C., & Botelheiro, A. A. (2021). The impact of intimate partner violence on psychological wellbeing: Predictors of posttraumatic stress disorder and the mediating role of insecure attachment styles. *European Journal of Trauma & Dissociation*, *5*(1), Article e100151. https://doi.org/10.1016/j.ejtd.2020.100151

Crocker, J., & Major, B. (1989). Social stigma and self-esteem: The self-protective properties of stigma. *Psychological Review*, *96*(4), 608–630. https://doi.org/10.1037/0033-295X.96.4.608

Cunradi, C. B., Caetano, R., & Schafer, J. (2002). Socioeconomic predictors of intimate partner violence among White, Black, and Hispanic couples in the United States. *Journal of Family Violence*, *17*(4), 377–389. https://doi.org/10.1023/A:1020374617328

D'Amore, C., Martin, S. L., Wood, K., & Brooks, C. (2018). Themes of healing and posttraumatic growth in women survivors' narratives of intimate partner violence. *Journal of Interpersonal Violence*, *36*(5–6), 1–28. https://doi.org/10.1177/0886260518767909

Darley, J. M., & Fazio, R. H. (1980). Expectancy confirmation processes arising in the social interaction sequence. *American Psychologist*, *35*(10), 867–881. https://doi.org/10.1037/0003-066X.35.10.867

Devries, K. M., Mak, J. Y., Bacchus, L. J. et al. (2013). Intimate partner violence and incident depressive symptoms and suicide attempts: A systematic review of longitudinal studies. *PLoS Medicine*, *10*(5), Article e1001439. https://doi.org/10.1271/journal.pmed.1001439

Dietrich, D. M., & Schuett, J. M. (2013). Culture of honor and attitudes toward intimate partner violence in Latinos. *SAGE Open*, *3*(2), 1–11. https://doi.org/10.1177/2158244013489685

Dillon, G., Hussain, R., Loxton, D., & Rahman, S. (2013). Mental and physical health and intimate partner violence against women: A review of the literature. *International Journal of Family Medicine, 2013*, Article e313909. https://doi.org/10.1155/2013/313909

Drigotas, S. M., Rusbult, C. E., Wieselquist, J., & Whitton, S. W. (1999). Close partner as sculptor of the ideal self: Behavioral affirmation and the Michelangelo phenomenon. *Journal of Personality and Social Psychology*, *77*(2), 293–323. https://doi.org/10.1037/0022-3514.77.2.293

Dumas, T. M., Lawford, H., Tieu, T., & Pratt, M. W. (2009). Positive parenting in adolescence and its relation to low point narration and identity status in emerging adulthood: A longitudinal analysis. *Developmental Psychology*, *45*(6), 1531–1544. https://doi.org/10.1037/a0017360

Dunlap, E., Golub, A., Johnson, B. D., & Wesley, D. (2002). Intergenerational transmission of conduct norms for drugs, sexual exploitation and violence: A case study. *British Journal of Criminology*, *42*(1), 1–20. https://doi.org/ 10.1093/bjc/42.1.1

Dutton, D. G. (1998). *The abusive personality: Violence and control in intimate relationships*. Guilford Press.

Dutton, D. G., & Painter, S. L. (1981). Traumatic bonding: The development of emotional attachments in battered women and other relationships of intermittent abuse. *Victimology: An International Journal*, *6*(1–4), 139–155.

Dutton, D. G., Saunders, K., Starzomski, A., & Bartholomew, K. (1994). Intimacy-anger and insecure attachment as precursors of abuse in intimate relationships. *Journal of Applied Social Psychology*, *24*, 1367–1386. https:// doi.org/10.1111/j.1559-1816.1994.tb01554.x

Eagly, A. H., Wood, W., & Johannesen-Schmidt, M. C. (2004). Social role theory of sex differences and similarities: Implications for the partner preferences of women and men. In A. H. Eagly, A. E. Beall, & R. J. Sternberg (Eds.), *The psychology of gender* (pp. 269–295). Guilford Press.

Elbert, T., Schauer, M., & Neuner, F. (2015). Narrative exposure therapy (NET): Reorganizing memories of traumatic stress, fear, and violence. In U. Schnyder & M. Cloitre (Eds.), *Evidence based treatments for trauma-related psychological disorders: A practical guide for clinicians* (pp. 229–253). Springer Switzerland.

Elderton, A., Berry, A., & Chan, C. (2017). A systematic review of posttraumatic growth in survivors of interpersonal violence in adulthood. *Trauma, Violence & Abuse*, *18*(2), 223–236. https://doi.org/10.1177/15248380 15611672

Estrellado, A. F., & Loh, J. M. I. (2014). Factors associated with battered Filipino women's decision to stay in or leave an abusive relationship. *Journal of Interpersonal Violence*, *29*(4), 575–592. https://doi.org/10.1177/ 0886260513505709

Fernández-Fuertes, A. A., Fernández-Rouco, N., Lázaro-Visa, S., & Gómez-Pérez, E. (2020). Myths about sexual aggression, sexual assertiveness and sexual violence in adolescent romantic relationships. *International Journal of Environmental Research and Public Health*, *17*(23), Article e8744. https:// doi.org/10.3390/ijerph17238744

Festinger, L., & Carlsmith, J. M. (1959). Cognitive consequences of forced compliance. *The Journal of Abnormal and Social Psychology, 58*(2), 203–210. https://doi.org/10.1037/h0041593

Finkel, E. J. (2008). Intimate partner violence perpetration: Insights from the science of self-regulation. In J. P. Forgas & J. Fitness (Eds.), *Social relationships: Cognitive, affective, and motivational processes* (pp. 271–288). Psychology Press.

Finkel, E. J. (2014). The I³ model: Metatheory, theory, and evidence. *Advances in Experimental Social Psychology, 49*, 1–104. https://doi.org/10.1016/B978-0-12-800052-6.00001-9

Finkel, E. J., DeWall, C. N., Slotter, E. B. et al. (2012). Using I³ theory to clarify when dispositional aggressiveness predicts intimate partner violence perpetration. *Journal of Personality and Social Psychology, 102*(3), 533–549. https://doi.org/10.1037/a0025651

Finkel, E. J., & Hall, A. N. (2018). The I³ model: A metatheoretical framework for understanding aggression. *Current Opinion in Psychology, 19*, 125–130. https://doi.org/10.1016/j.copsyc.2017.03.013

Flasch, P., Fall, K., Stice, B. et al. (2020). Messages to new survivors by longer-term survivors of intimate partner violence. *Journal of Family Violence, 35*, 29–41. https://doi.org/10.1007/s10896-019-00078-8

Foa, E. B. (2011). Prolonged exposure therapy: Past, present, and future. *Depression and Anxiety, 28*(12), 1043–1047. https://doi.org/10.1002/da.20907

Follingstad, D. R., Neckerman, A. P., & Vormbrock, J. (1988). Reactions to victimization and coping strategies of battered women: The ties that bind. *Clinical Psychology Review, 8*(4), 373–390. https://doi.org/10.1016/0272-7358(88)90065-7

Fugate, M., Landis, L., Riordan, K. et al. (2005). Barriers to domestic violence help seeking implications for intervention. *Violence against Women, 11*(3), 290–310. https://doi.org/10.1177/1077801204271959

Gilbert, D. T., Pinel, E. C., Wilson, T. D., Blumberg, S. J., & Wheatley, T. P. (1998). Immune neglect: A source of durability bias in affective forecasting. *Journal of Personality and Social Psychology, 75*(3), 617–638. https://doi.org/10.1037/0022-3514.75.3.617

Giles-Sims, J. (1998). *The aftermath of partner violence.* Sage.

Gonçalves, O. (2002). *Viver narrativamente: A psicoterapia como adjectivação da experiência* [*Living narratively: Psychotherapy as an adjectivation of experience*]. Quarteto.

Gonçalves, O., & Machado, P. (1999). Cognitive narrative psychotherapy: Research foundations. *Journal of Clinical Psychology, 55*(10), 1179–1191.

https://doi.org/10.1002/(SICI)1097-4679(199910)55:10<1179::AID-JCLP2>3.0.CO;2-L

Goodfriend, W., & Agnew, C. R. (2008). Sunken costs and desired plans: Examining different types of investments in close relationships. *Personality and Social Psychology Bulletin, 34*(12), 1639–1652. https://doi.org/10.1177/0146167208323743

Goodfriend, W., & Arriaga, X. B. (2018). Cognitive reframing of intimate partner aggression: Social and contextual influences. *International Journal of Environmental Research and Public Health, 15,* 115. https://doi.org/10.3390/ijerph15112464

Goodkind, J. R., Gillum, T. L., Bybee, D. I., & Sullivan, C. M. (2003). The impact of family and friends' reactions on the well-being of women with abusive partners. *Violence against Women, 9*(3), 347–373. https://doi.org/10.1177/1077801202250083

Goodman, L. A., & Epstein, D. (2008). *Listening to battered women: A survivor-centered approach to advocacy, mental health, and justice.* American Psychological Association.

Greenwald, A. G., Banaji, M. R., Rudman, L. A. et al. (2002). A unified theory of implicit attitudes, stereotypes, self-esteem, and self-concept. *Psychological Review, 109*(1), 3–25. https://doi.org/10.1037/0033-295X.109.1.3

Hague, G., Mullender, A., & Aris, R. (2003). *Is anyone listening? Accountability and women survivors of domestic violence.* Psychology Press.

Hamilton, M. C., Anderson, D., Broaddus, M., & Young, K. (2006). Gender stereotyping and underrepresentation of female characters in 200 popular children's picture books: A twenty-first century update. *Sex Roles, 55*(11–12), 757–765. https://doi.org/10.1007/s11199-006-9128-6

Hammett, J. F., Karney, B. R., & Bradbury, T. N. (2020). Adverse childhood experiences, stress, and intimate partner violence among newlywed couples living with low incomes. *Journal of Family Psychology, 34*(4), 436–447. https://doi.org/10.1037/fam0000629

Helgeson, V. S., Reynolds, K. A., & Tomich, P. L. (2006). A meta-analytic review of benefit finding and growth. *Journal of Consulting and Clinical Psychology, 74*(5), 797–816. https://doi.org/10.1037/0022-006X.74.5.797

Helloflo.com. (2021). *"Survivor" versus "victim": Why choosing your words carefully is important.* https://helloflo.com/survivor-vs-victim-why-choosing-your-words-carefully-isimportant/

Hendrika, M., Hampton, M., & Bruyninx, S. (2012, October). *Summary of healing journey presentations/analyses conducted in Saskatchewan.* Presented at RESOLVE Research Day, Regina, Saskatchewan, Canada.

Henriksen, C. B., Mattick, K. L., & Fisher, B. S. (2015). Mandatory bystander intervention training: Is the Save Act requirement the "right" program to reduce violence among college students? In S. Carrigan Wooten & R. W. Mitchell (Eds.), *The crisis of campus sexual violence* (pp. 169–183). Routledge.

Herzberger, S. D., & Rueckert, Q. H. (1997). Attitudes as explanations for aggression against family members. In G. K. Kantor & J. L. Jasinski (Eds.), *Out of the darkness: Contemporary perspectives on family violence* (pp. 151–160). Sage.

Heywood, I., Sammut, D., & Bradbury-Jones, C. (2019). A qualitative exploration of "thrivership" among women who have experienced domestic violence and abuse: Development of a new model. *BMC Women's Health, 19*(1), 1–15.

Higgins, E. T. (1987). Self-discrepancy: A theory relating self and affect. *Psychological Review, 94*(3), 319–340. https://doi.org/10.1037/0033-295X.94.3.319

Hoerger, M., Quirk, S. W., Lucas, R. E., & Carr, T. H. (2010). Cognitive determinants of affective forecasting errors. *Judgment and Decision Making, 5*(5), 365–373. https://doi.org/10.1037/t38798-000

Holtzworth-Munroe, A., & Meehan, J. C. (2004). Typologies of men who are maritally violent: Scientific and clinical implications. *Journal of Interpersonal Violence, 19*(12), 1369–1389. https://doi.org/10.1177/0886260504269693

Holtzworth-Munroe, A., Meehan, J. C., Herron, K., Rehman, U., & Stuart, G. L. (2000). Testing the Holtzworth-Munroe and Stuart (1994) batterer typology. *Journal of Consulting and Clinical Psychology, 68*(6), 1000–1019. https://doi.org/10.1037/0022-006X.68.6.1000

Holtzworth-Munroe, A., & Stuart, G. L. (1994). Typologies of male batterers: Three subtypes and the differences among them. *Psychological Bulletin, 116*(3), 476–497. https://doi.org/10.1037/00332909.116.3.476

Hou, W.-L., Ko, N.-Y., & Shu, B.-C. (2013). Recovery experiences of Taiwanese women after terminating abusive relationships: A phenomenology study. *Journal of Interpersonal Violence, 28*(1), 157–175. https://doi.org/10.1177/0886260512448851

House, J. (1981). *Work stress and social support*. Addison-Wesley.

Jackson, S. (2001). Happily never after: Young women's stories of abuse in heterosexual love relationships. *Feminism & Psychology, 11*(3), 305–321. https://doi.org/10.1177/0959353501011003004

Jacobson, N. S., & Gottman, J. M. (1998). *When men batter women: New insights into ending abusive relationships*. Simon & Schuster.

Jaffray, B. (2021). Intimate partner violence: Experiences of sexual minority women in Canada, 2018. *Juristat: Canadian Centre for Justice Statistics*, *1*, 3–18. www150.statcan.gc.ca/n1/pub/85-002-x/2021001/article/00005-eng.htm

Janoff-Bulman, R. (1992). *Shattered assumptions: Towards a new psychology of trauma*. Free Press.

Janoff-Bulman, R. (2006). Schema-change perspectives on posttraumatic growth. In L. G. Calhoun & R. G. Tedeschi (Eds.), *Handbook of posttraumatic growth: Research and practice* (pp. 81–99). Lawrence Erlbaum.

Janoff-Bulman, R., & Yopyk, D. J. (2004). Random outcomes and valued commitments. In J. Greenberg, S. L. Koole, & T. Pyszczynski (Eds.), *Handbook of experimental existential psychology* (pp. 122–138). Guilford Press.

Jenks, K. (2014). *How women experience post-traumatic growth as survivors of intimate partner violence: An interpretative phenomenological analysis* (ID No. uj:14484) [Doctoral dissertation, University of Johannesburg]. University of Johannesburg Institutional Repository. https://ujcontent.uj.ac .za/%20vital/access/manager/Repository/uj:14484?view=null&f0=sm_con tributor%3A%22Du+Plessis%2C+L.%22&sort=sort_ss_sm_creator+desc

Johnson, M. P. (1995). Patriarchal terrorism and common couple violence: Two forms of violence against women. *Journal of Marriage and the Family*, *57*(2), 283–294. https://doi.org/10.2307/353683

Johnson, M. P. (2007). The intersection of gender and control. In L. O'Toole, J. R. Schiffman, & M. L. K. Edwards (Eds.), *Gender violence: Interdisciplinary perspectives* (2nd ed., pp. 257–268). New York University Press.

Joireman, J., Parrott, L., & Hammersla, J. (2002). Empathy and the self-absorption paradox: Support for the distinction between self-rumination and self-reflection. *Self and Identity*, *1*(1), 53–65. https://doi.org/10.1080/ 152988602317232803

Jordan, J. V. (2003). Relational-cultural therapy. In M. Kopala & M. A. Keitel (Eds.), *Handbook of counseling women* (pp. 22–30). Sage.

Kelley, H. H., & Thibaut, J. W. (1978). *Interpersonal relations: A theory of interdependence*. Wiley.

Kernic, M. A., Monary-Ernsdorff, D. J., Koespell, J. K., & Holt, V. L. (2005). Children in the crossfire: Child custody determinations against couples with a history of intimate partner violence. *Violence against Women*, *11*(8), 991–1021. https://doi.org/10.177/1077801205278042

Kimmes, J. G., Mallory, A. B., Spencer, C. et al. (2019). A meta-analysis of risk markers for intimate partner violence in same-sex relationships. *Trauma, Violence, & Abuse*, *20*(3), 374–384. https://doi.org/10.1177/152483801 7708784

Kirkwood, C. (1993). *Leaving abusive partners: From the scars of survival to the wisdom for change.* Sage.

Knapp, D. (2019). Fanning the flames: Gaslighting as tactic of psychological abuse and criminal prosecution. *Albany Law Review, 83*(1), 313–337. https://heinonline.org/HOL/Page?handle=hein.journals/albany83&div=13&g_sent=1&casa_token=

Ko, Y., & Park, S. (2020). Building a new intimate relationship after experiencing intimate partner violence in victim-survivors of South Korea. *Journal of Interpersonal Violence, 35*(1–2), 3–24. https://doi.org/10.1177/0886260518814265

Kurz, D. (1995). *For richer, for poorer: Mothers confront divorce.* Routledge.

Leadership Council on Child Abuse and Interpersonal Violence. (2008). *How many children are court-ordered into unsupervised contact with an abusive parent after divorce?* https://leadershipcouncil.org/1/med/PR3html

Levinson, C. A., & Rodebaugh, T. L. (2013). Anxiety, self-discrepancy, and regulatory focus theory: Acculturation matters. *Anxiety, Stress & Coping, 26*(2), 171–186. https://doi.org/10.1080/10615806.2012.659728

Liang, B., Goodman, L., Tummala-Narra, P., & Weintraub, S. (2005). A theoretical framework for understanding help-seeking processes among survivors of intimate partner violence. *American Journal of Community Psychology, 36*(1–2), 71–84. https://doi.org/10.1007/s10464-005-6233-6

Linley, P. A., & Joseph, S. (2004). Positive change following trauma and adversity: A review. *Journal of Traumatic Stress, 17*(1), 11–21. https://doi.org/10.1023/B:JOTS.0000014671.27856.7e

Littleton, H. (2010). The impact of social support and negative disclosure reaction on sexual assault victims: A cross-sectional and longitudinal investigation. *Journal of Trauma & Dissociation, 11*(2), 210–227. https://doi.org/10.1080/15299730903502946

Lowe, M., Khan, R., Thanzami, V., Barzy, M., & Karmaliani, R. (2018). Attitudes toward intimate partner "honor"-based violence in India, Iran, Malaysia and Pakistan. *Journal of Aggression, Conflict and Peace Research, 10*(4), 283–292. https://doi.org/10.1108/JACPR-09-2017-0324

Machado, A., Santos, A., Graham-Kevan, N., & Matos, M. (2017). Exploring help seeking experiences of male victims of female perpetrators of IPV. *Journal of Family Violence, 32*(5), 513–523. https://doi.org/10.1007/s10896-016-9853-8

Macy, R. J., Ferron, J., & Crosby, C. (2009). Partner violence and survivors' chronic health problems: Informing social work practice. *Social Work, 54*(1), 29–43. https://doi.org/10.1093/sw/54.1.29

Maier, S. F., & Seligman, M. E. (1976). Learned helplessness: Theory and evidence. *Journal of Experimental Psychology: General, 105*(1), 3–46. https://doi.org/10.1037/0096-3445.105.1.3

Marín-Morales, A., Bueso-Izquierdo, N., Hidalgo-Ruzzante, N. et al. (2020). "Would you allow your wife to dress in a miniskirt to the party"? Batterers do not activate default mode network during moral decisions about intimate partner violence. *Journal of Interpersonal Violence*, [online], 1–26. https://doi.org/10.1177/0886260520926494

Masanet, M. J., Medina-Bravo, P., & Ferrés, J. (2018). Myths of romantic love and gender-based violence in the fan forum of the Spanish teen series Los Protegidos. *Young, 26*(4), 96S–112S. https://doi.org/10.1177/1103308817748432

Matheson, F. I., Daoud, N., Hamilton-Wright, S. et al. (2015). Where did she go? The transformation of self-esteem, self-identity, and mental well-being among women who have experienced intimate partner violence. *Women's Health Issues, 25*(5), 561–569. https://doi.org/10.1016/jwhi.2015.04.006

McLindon, E., Humphreys, C., & Hegarty, K. (2018). "It happens to clinicians too": An Australian prevalence study of intimate partner and family violence against health professionals. *BMC Women's Health, 18*(1), 1–7. https://doi.org/10.1186/s12905-018-0588-y

Merton, R. K. (1948). The self-fulfilling prophecy. *The Antioch Review, 8*(2), 193–210. https://doi.org/10.2307/4609267

Messinger, A. M. (2011). Invisible victims: Same-sex IPV in the national violence against women survey. *Journal of Interpersonal Violence, 26*(11), 2228–2243. https://doi.org/10.1177/0886260510383023

Metz, C., Calmet, J., & Thevenot, A. (2019). Women subjected to domestic violence: The impossibility of separation. *Psychoanalytic Psychology, 36*(1), 36–43. https://doi.org/10.1037/pap0000186

Mookerjee, S., Cerulli, C., Fernandez, I. D., & Chin, N. P. (2015). Do Hispanic and non-Hispanic women survivors of intimate partner violence differ in regards to their help-seeking? A qualitative study. *Journal of Family Violence, 30*, 839–851. https://doi.org/10.1007/s10896-0159734-6

Moreira, A., Moreira, A. C., & Rocha, J. C. (2020). Randomized controlled trial: Cognitive-narrative therapy for IPV victims. *Journal of Interpersonal Violence*, [online], 1–17. https://doi.org/10.1177/0886260520943719

Moss, V. A., Pitula, C. R., Campbell, J. C., & Halstead, L. (1997). The experience of terminating an abusive relationship from an Anglo and African American perspective: A qualitative descriptive study. *Issues in Mental Health Nursing, 18*(5), 433–454. https://doi.org/10.3109/01612849709009423

Murray, C. E., Crowe, A., & Overstreet, N. M. (2018). Sources and components of stigma experienced by survivors of intimate partner violence. *Journal of Interpersonal Violence, 33*(3), 515–536. https://doi.org/10.1177/08862605 15609565

Nathanson, A. M., Shorey, R. C., Tirone, V., & Rhatigan, D. L. (2012). The prevalence of mental health disorders in a community sample of female victims of intimate partner violence. *Partner Abuse, 3*(1), 59–75. https://doi.org/10.1891/1946-6560.3.1.59

National Center for Victims of Crime. (2018). *2018 NCVRW Resource Guide: Intimate partner violence fact sheet.* https://ovc.ojp.gov/sites/g/files/xyckuh226/files/ncvrw2018/info_flyers/fact_sheets/2018NCVRW_IPV_508_QC.pdf

National Coalition Against Domestic Violence. (2020). Domestic violence. https://assets.speakcdn.com/assets/2497/domestic_violence-20200807093 50855.pdf?1596828650457

National Coalition Against Domestic Violence. (2021). *50 obstacles to leaving.* www.thehotline.org/resources/get-help-50-obstacles-to-leaving/

Njie-Carr, V. P., Sabri, B., Messing, J. T. et al. (2020). Understanding intimate partner violence among immigrant and refugee women: A grounded theory analysis. *Journal of Aggression, Maltreatment & Trauma,* [online], 1–19. https://doi.org/10.1080/10926771.2020.1796870

O'Doherty, L. J., Taft, A., McNair, R., & Hegarty, K. (2016). Fractured identity in the context of intimate partner violence: Barriers to and opportunities for seeking help in health settings. *Violence against Women, 22*(2), 225–248. https://doi.org/10.1177/1077801215601248

Olson, L. N. (2004). The role of voice in the (re) construction of a battered woman's identity: An autoethnography of one woman's experiences of abuse. *Women's Studies in Communication, 27*(1), 1–33. https://doi.org/10.1080/07491409.2004.10162464

Orang, T., Ayoughi, S., Moran, J. K. et al. (2018). The efficacy of narrative exposure therapy in a sample of Iranian women exposed to ongoing intimate partner violence – A randomized controlled trial. *Clinical Psychology & Psychotherapy, 25*(6), 1–15. https://doi.org/10.1002/cpp.2318

Overstreet, N. M., & Quinn, D. M. (2013). The intimate partner violence stigmatization model and barriers to help seeking. *Basic and Applied Social Psychology, 35*(1), 109–122. https://doi.org/10.1080/01973533.2012.746599

Parra-Barrera, S. M., Moyano, N., Boldova, M. Á., & Sánchez-Fuentes, M. D. M. (2021). Protection against sexual violence in the Colombian legal framework: Obstacles and consequences for women victims. *International Journal of*

Environmental Research and Public Health, 18(8), Article 4171. https://doi .org/10.3390/ijerph18084171

Peitzmeier, S. M., Malik, M., Kattari, S. K. et al. (2020). Intimate partner violence in transgender populations: Systematic review and meta-analysis of prevalence and correlates. *American Journal of Public Health, 110*(9), e1– e14. https://doi.org/10.2105/AJPH.2020.305774

Pence, E. (2001). Advocacy on behalf of battered women. In C. M. Renzetti, J. L. Edleson, & R. K. Bergen (Eds.), *Sourcebook on violence against women* (pp. 329–343). Sage.

Pence, E., & Paymar, M. (1993). *Education groups for men who batter: The Duluth model.* Springer.

Pennebaker, J. W. (1997). Writing about emotional experiences as a therapeutic process. *Psychological Science, 8*(3), 162–166. https://doi.org/10.1111/ j.1467-9280.1997.tb00403.x

Pereira, M. E., Azeredo, A., Moreira, D., Brandão, I., & Almeida, F. (2020). Personality characteristics of victims of intimate partner violence: A systematic review. *Aggression and Violent Behavior, 52*, Article e101423. https://doi.org/10.1016/j.avb.2020.101423

Peterson, C., & Seligman, M. E. P. (1983). Learned helplessness and victimization. *Journal of Social Issues, 39*(2), 103–116. https://doi.org/ 10.1111/j.1540-4560.1983.tb00143.x

Pittman, D. M., Riedy Rush, C., Hurley, K. B., & Minges, M. L. (2020). Double jeopardy: Intimate partner violence vulnerability among emerging adult women through lenses of race and sexual orientation. *Journal of American College Health*, [online], 1–9. https://doi.org/10.1080/07448481.2020 .1740710

Prentice, D. A., & Carranza, E. (2002). What women and men should be, shouldn't be, are allowed to be, and don't have to be: The contents of prescriptive gender stereotypes. *Psychology of Women Quarterly, 26*(4), 269–281. https://doi.org/10.1111/1471-6402.t01-1-00066

Rivenburgh, N. K. (2000). Social identity theory and news portrayals of citizens involved in international affairs. *Media Psychology, 2*(4), 303–329. https:// doi.org/10.1207/S1532785XMEP0204_01

Rizkalla, K., Maar, M., Pilon, R., McGregor, L., & Reade, M. (2020). Improving the response of primary care providers to rural First Nation women who experience intimate partner violence: A qualitative study. *BMC Women's Health, 20*(1), 1–13. https://doi.org/10.1186/s12905-020- 01053y

Roberts, A. R., & Roberts, B. J. (1981). *Sheltering battered women: A national study and service guide.* Springer.

Rodriguez, M., Valentine, J. M., Son, J. B., & Marjani, M. (2010). Intimate partner violence and barriers to mental care for ethnically diverse populations of women. *Trauma Violence Abuse*, *10*(4), 358–374. https://doi.org/10.1177/1524838009339756

Rolling, E. S., & Brosi, M. W. (2010). A multi-level and integrated approach to assessment and intervention of intimate partner violence. *Journal of Family Violence*, *25*, 229–236. https://doi.org/10.1007/s10896-009-9286-8

Romero-Sánchez, M., Skowronski, M., Bohner, G., & Megías, J. L. (2020). Talking about "victims," "survivors" and "battered women": How labels affect the perception of women who have experienced intimate partner violence. *International Journal of Social Psychology*, [online], 3060. https://doi.org/10.1080/02134748.2020.1840232

Rosen, K. H. (1996). The ties that bind women to violent premarital relationships: Processes of seduction and entrapment. In D. D. Cahn & S. A. Lloyd (Eds.), *Family violence from a communication perspective* (pp. 151–176). Sage.

Rosen, K. H., & Stith, S. M. (1997). Surviving abusive dating relationships: Processes of leaving, healing and moving on. In G. Kantor & J. Jasinski (Eds.), *Out of the darkness: Contemporary perspectives on family violence* (pp. 170–182). Sage.

Roth, S., & Lebowitz, L. (1988). The experience of sexual trauma. *Journal of Traumatic Stress*, *1*(1), 79–107. https://doi.org/10.1002/jts.2490010107

Rotter, J. B. (1966). Generalized expectancies for internal versus external control of reinforcement. *Psychological Monographs: General and Applied*, *80*(1), 1–28. https://doi.org/10.1037/h0092976

Rotter, J. B. (1975). Some problems and misconceptions related to the construct of internal versus external control of reinforcement. *Journal of Consulting and Clinical Psychology*, *43*(1), 56–67. https://doi.org/10.1037/h0076301

Rudman, L. A., & Heppen, J. B. (2003). Implicit romantic fantasies and women's interest in personal power: A glass slipper effect? *Personality and Social Psychology Bulletin*, *29*(11), 1357–1370. https://doi.org/10.1177/0146167203256906

Rusbult, C. E., & Martz, J. M. (1995). Remaining in an abusive relationship: An investment model analysis of nonvoluntary dependence. *Personality and Social Psychology Bulletin*, *21*(6), 558–571. https://doi.org/10.1177/0146167295216002

Sabourin, T. C. (1995). The role of negative reciprocity in spouse abuse: A relational control analysis. *Journal of Applied Communication Research*, *23*(4), 271–283. https://doi.org/10.1080/00909889509365431

Saccuzzo, D. P., & Johnson, N. E. (2004). Child custody mediation's failure to protect: Why should the criminal justice system care? *National Institute of Justice Journal, 251,* 21–23. https://nij.ojp.gov/library/publications/child-custody-mediations-failure-protect-whyshould-criminal-justice-system

Sáez, G., López-Nuñez, C., Carlos-Vivas, J. et al. (2021). A multicomponent program to improve self-concept and self-esteem among intimate partner violence victims: A study protocol for a randomized controlled pilot trial. *International Journal of Environmental Research and Public Health, 18*(9), Article e4930. https://doi.org/10.3390/ijerph18094930

Sáez, G., Riemer, A. R., Brock, R. L., & Gervais, S. J. (2020). The role of interpersonal sexual objectification in heterosexual intimate partner violence from perspectives of perceivers and targets. *Journal of Interpersonal Violence,* [online], 1–26. https://doi.org/10.1177/0886260520922348

Sánchez-Hernández, M. D., Herrera-Enríquez, M. C., & Expósito, F. (2020). Controlling behaviors in couple relationships in the digital age: Acceptability of gender violence, sexism, and myths about romantic love. *Psychosocial Intervention, 29*(2), 67–81. https://doi.org/10.5093/pi2020a1

Sauber, E. W., & O'Brien, K. M. (2020). Multiple losses: The psychological and economic well-being of survivors of intimate partner violence. *Journal of Interpersonal Violence, 35*(15–16), 3054–3078. https://doi.org/10.1177/0886260517706760

Savage, L. (2021). Intimate partner violence: Experiences of women with disabilities in Canada, 2018. *Juristat: Canadian Centre for Justice Statistics, 1,* 3–23. https://www150.statcan.gc.ca/n1/pub/85-002-x/2021001/article/00006-eng.htm

Schauer, M., Neuner, F., & Elbert, T. (2011). *Narrative exposure therapy: A short-term treatment for traumatic stress disorders* (2nd ed.). Hogrefe.

Schechter, S. (1982). *Women and male violence: The visions and struggles of the battered women's movement.* South End Press.

Scheer, J. R., Martin-Storey, A., & Baams, L. (2020). Help-seeking barriers among sexual and gender minority individuals who experience intimate partner violence victimization. In B. Russell (Ed.), *Intimate partner violence and the LGBT+ community* (pp. 139–158). Springer. https://doi.org/10.1007/978-3-030-44762-5_8

Seligman, M. E. (1972). Learned helplessness. *Annual Review of Medicine, 23* (1), 407–412.

Seligman, M. E. P., & Csikszentmihalyi, M. (2000). Positive psychology: An introduction. *American Psychologist, 55*(1), 5–14. https://doi.org/10.1037/0003-066X.55.1.5

Senkans, S., McEwan, T. E., & Ogloff, J. R. (2020). Conceptualising intimate partner violence perpetrators' cognition as aggressive relational schemas. *Aggression and Violent Behavior*, [online], Article e101456. https://doi.org/10.1016/j.avb.2020.101456

Senn, C. Y., & Forrest, A. (2016). "And then one night when I went to class . . . ": The impact of sexual assault bystander intervention workshops incorporated in academic courses. *Psychology of Violence*, *6*(4), 607–618. https://doi.org/10.1037/a0039660

Senter, K. E., & Caldwell, K. (2002). Spirituality and the maintenance of change: A phenomenological study of women who leave abusive relationships. *Contemporary Family Therapy*, *24*, 543–564. https://doi.org/10.1023/a:1021269028756

Sharma-Patel, K., Brown, E. J., & Chaplin, W. F. (2012). Emotional and cognitive processing in sexual assault survivors' narratives. *Journal of Aggression, Maltreatment & Trauma*, *21*(2), 149–170. https://doi.org/10.1080/10926771.2012.639053

Sherif, M. (1966). *In common predicament: Social psychology of intergroup conflict and cooperation*. Houghton Mifflin.

Silberg, J., & Dallam, S. (2019). Abusers gaining custody in family courts: A case series of over turned decisions. *Journal of Child Custody*, *16*(2), 140–169. https://doi.org/10.1080/15379418.2019.1613204

Slattery, S. M., & Goodman, L. A. (2009). Secondary traumatic stress among domestic violence advocates: Workplace risk and protective factors. *Violence against Women*, *15*(11), 1358–1379. https://doi.org/10.1177/1077801209347469

Song, L. (2012). Service utilization, perceived changes of self, and life satisfaction among women who experienced intimate partner abuse: The mediation effect of empowerment. *Journal of Interpersonal Violence*, *27*(6), 1112–1136. https://doi.org/10.1177/0886260511424495

Stalans, L. J., & Ritchie, J. (2008). Relationship of substance use/abuse with psychological and physical intimate partner violence: Variations across living situations. *Journal of Family Violence*, *23*(1), 9–24. https://doi.org/10.1007/s10896-007-9125-8

Stern, E., van der Heijden, I., & Dunkle, K. (2020). How people with disabilities experience programs to prevent intimate partner violence across four countries. *Evaluation and Program Planning*, *79*, Article e101770. https://doi.org/10.1016/j.evalprogplan.2019.101770

Stith, S. M., Rosen, K. H., Middleton, K. A. et al. (2000). The intergenerational transmission of spouse abuse: A meta-analysis. *Journal of Marriage and Family*, *62*(3), 640–654. https://doi.org/10.1111/j.1741-3737.2000.00640.x

Street, A. E., & Arias, I. (2001). Psychological abuse and posttraumatic stress disorder in battered women: Examining the roles of shame and guilt. *Violence and Victims*, *16*(1), 65–78. https://doi.org/10.1891/0886-6708.16.1.65

St. Vil, N. M., Carter, T., & Johnson, S. (2021). Betrayal trauma and barriers to forming new intimate relationships among survivors of intimate partner violence. *Journal of Interpersonal Violence*, *36*(7–8), NP3495–NP3509. https://doi.org/10.1177/0886260518779596

Sweet, P. L. (2019). The sociology of gaslighting. *American Sociological Review*, *84*(5), 851–875. https://doi.org/10.1177/0003122419874843

Tajfel, H. M. (1981). *Human groups and social categories: Studies in social psychology*. Cambridge University Press Archive.

Tajfel, H. M. (1982). Social psychology of intergroup relations. *Annual Review of Psychology*, *33*(1), 1–39. https://doi.org/10.1146/annurev.ps.33.020182 .000245

Tarzia, L. (2021a). "It went to the very heart of who I was as a woman": The invisible impacts of intimate partner sexual violence. *Qualitative Health Research*, *31*(2), 287–297. https://doi.org/10.1177/1049732320967659

Tarzia, L. (2021b). Toward an ecological understanding of intimate partner sexual violence. *Journal of Interpersonal Violence*, *36*(23–24), 11704–11727. https://doi.org/10.1177/0886260519900298

Taylor, J. Y. (2004). Moving from surviving to thriving: African American women recovering from intimate male partner abuse. *Research and Theory for Nursing Practice*, *18*(1), 35–50. https://doi.org/10.1891/rtnp.18.1.35.28056

Taylor, S. E. (2011). Social support: A review. In M. S. Friedman (Ed.), *The handbook of health psychology* (pp. 189–214). Oxford University Press.

Tedeschi, R. G., & Calhoun, L. G. (1995). *Trauma and transformation: Growing in the aftermath of suffering*. Sage.

Tedeschi, R. G., & Calhoun, L. G. (1996). The posttraumatic growth inventory: Measuring the positive legacy of trauma. *Journal of Traumatic Stress*, *9*(3), 455–471. https://doi.org/10.1002/jts.2490090305

Tedeschi, R. G., & Calhoun, L. G. (2004a). Posttraumatic growth: Conceptual foundations and empirical evidence. *Psychological Inquiry*, *15*(1), 1–18. https://doi.org/10.1207//s15327965pli1501_01

Tedeschi, R. G., & Calhoun, L. G. (2004b). The foundations of posttraumatic growth: New considerations. *Psychological Inquiry*, *15*(1), 93–102. https://doi.org/10.1207/s15327965pli1501_03

Tedeschi, R. G., Shakespeare-Finch, J., Taku, K., & Calhoun, L. G. (2018). *Posttraumatic growth: Theory, research, and applications*. Routledge.

Tutty, L., Radtke, H. L., & Nixon, K. L. (2009). *The healing journey: A longitudinal study of mothers affected by intimate partner violence, perceptions of their children's well-being and family-related service utilization*. Alberta Centre for Child, Family and Community Research. www2 .uregina.ca/resolve/assets/pdf/TuttyReport.pdf

Ubillos-Landa, S., Puente-Martínez, A., González-Castro, J. L. et al. (2020). You belong to me! Meta-analytic review of the use of male control and dominance against women in intimate partner violence. *Aggression and Violent Behavior, 52*, Article e101392. https://doi.org/10.1016/j.avb.2020 .101392

Ulloa, E. C., Hammett, J. F., Guzman, M. L., & Hokoda, A. (2015). Psychological growth in relation to intimate partner violence: A review. *Aggression and Violent Behavior, 25*(A), 88–94. https://doi.org/10.1016/ j.avb.2015.07.007

Valdez, C. E., & Lilly, M. M. (2015). Posttraumatic growth in survivors of intimate partner violence: An assumptive world process. *Journal of Interpersonal Violence, 30*(2), 215–231. https://doi.org/10.1177/088626051 4533154

Volpe, E. M., Quinn, C. R., Resch, K. et al. (2017). Narrative exposure therapy: A proposed model to address IPV-related PTSD in parenting and pregnant adolescents. *Family Community Health, 40*(3), 258–277. https://doi.org/ 10.1097/FCH.0000000000000072

Walker, L. A. (1984). Battered women, psychology, and public policy. *American Psychologist, 39*(10), 1178–1182. https://doi.org/10.1037/0003- 066X.39.10.1178

Wies, J. R. (2008). Professionalizing human services: A case of domestic violence shelter advocates. *Human Organization, 67*(2), 221–233. https:// doi.org/10.17730/humo.67.2.143m2v5421171113

Welldon, E. V. (2011). Perverse transference and the malignant bonding. In E. V. Welldon (Ed.), *Playing with dynamite: A personal approach to the psychoanalytic understanding of perversions, violence and criminality* (pp. 50–59). Karnac Books.

West, C. M. (1998). Leaving a second closet: Outing partner violence in same- sex couples. In J. L. Jasinski & L. M. Williams (Eds.), *Partner violence: A comprehensive review of 20 years of research* (pp. 163–183). Sage.

Wood, L. (2017). "I look across from me and I see me": Survivors as advocates in intimate partner violence agencies. *Violence against Women, 23*(3), 309–329. https://doi.org/10.1177/1077801216641518

World Health Organization. (2010). *Preventing intimate partner and sexual violence against women: Taking action and generating evidence*. www.who .int/violence_injury_prevention/publications/violence/9789241564007_eng .pdf

Zapor, H., Wolford-Clevenger, C., & Johnson, D. M. (2015). The association between social support and stages of change in survivors of intimate partner violence. *Journal of Interpersonal Violence*, *33*(7), 1051–1070. https://doi.org/10.1177/0886260515614282

Zukauskiene, R., Kaniusonyte, G., Bergman, L. R., Bakaityte, A., & Truskauskaite-Kuneviciene, I. (2021). The role of social support in identity processes and posttraumatic growth: A study of victims of intimate partner violence. *Journal of Interpersonal Violence*, *36*(15–16), 7599–7624. https://doi.org/10.1177/0886260519836785

Cambridge Elements ☰

Applied Social Psychology

Susan Clayton
College of Wooster, Ohio

Susan Clayton is a social psychologist at the College of Wooster in Wooster, Ohio. Her research focuses on the human relationship with nature, how it is socially constructed, and how it can be utilized to promote environmental concern.

About the Series

Many social psychologists have used their research to understand and address pressing social issues, from poverty and prejudice to work and health. Each Element in this series reviews a particular area of applied social psychology. Elements will also discuss applications of the research findings and describe directions for future study.

Cambridge Elements ☰

Applied Social Psychology

Elements in the Series

A full series listing is available at: www.cambridge.org/EASP

Printed in the United States
by Baker & Taylor Publisher Services